Spicy Cajun Cooking

Master the Art of Cajun Cuisine with These Mouth-Watering and Authentic 100 Delicious Recipes to Bring the Flavors of Louisiana to Your Kitchen

Richard Harrison

Copyright Material ©2023

All Rights Reserved

Without the proper written consent of the publisher and copyright owner, this book cannot be used or distributed in any way, shape, or form, except for brief quotations used in a review. This book should not be considered a substitute for medical, legal, or other professional advice.

TABLE OF CONTENTS

TABLE OF CONTENTS 3
INTRODUCTION 6
GUMBO 7
   1. Jamaican Squash Soup 8
   2. Keto egg drop soup 11
   3. Jamaican shrimp soup 13
   4. Stewed Calaloo 15
   5. Coconut Prawn Soup 17
   6. Gungo Pea Soup 20
   7. Instant Pot Lentil Gumbo 22
   8. Alaska octopus gumbo 24
   9. Baked vegetable gumbo creole 26
   10. Cajun catfish gumbo 29
JAMBALAYA 31
   11. Slow Cooker Jambalaya 32
   12. Red Bean Jambalaya 34
   13. Baked Jambalaya Casserole 36
   14. Sausage Jambalaya 38
   15. Chicken Jambalaya with Sausage 40
   16. Jambalaya-Stuffed Cabbage Rolls 42
   17. Quinoa jambalaya 45
   18. Alligator jambalaya 47
   19. Bayou boeuf jambalaya 49
   20. Black-eyed peas and sausage jambalaya 51
RED BEANS AND RICE 53
   21. Long-grain Rice and pinto bean 54
   22. Lime chicken with egg-fried long-grain rice 56
   23. Long-grain Rice Hoppin' John 59
   24. Mexican-Inspired Pinto Beans and Rice 61
   25. Pinto Beans and Rice with Cilantro 63
   26. Spanish Pinto Beans & Rice 66
   27. One-Pot Rice and Beans 69
   28. Southern Pinto Beans and Rice 71
   29. Pinto Beans and Rice and Sausage 73
   30. Gallopinto (Nicaraguan Rice and Beans) 75
   31. Bean sauce & tomatoes over rice 78
   32. Cajun pinto beans 81
   33. Rice & beans with cheese 83

34. Pinto Beans and Saffron Rice 85
35. Taco Seasoning rice with pinto beans 87
36. Indian pumpkin rice and beans 89
37. Mexican Cowboy Beans 91
38. Caribbean Feast 93
39. Jamaican Jerk Jackfruit & Beans with Rice 96
40. Rice Pilaf With Bean, Fruits And Nuts 99
41. Beans and rice cha cha cha bowl 101
42. Turnip Stir Fry with Beans 103
43. Rice with lamb, dill and beans 105
44. Cheesy Pinto Beans 108
45. Rice and beans with basil pesto 110
46. Flank steak with black beans and rice 112
47. African Rice and Beans 115
48. Tumbleweed, pinto bean, and rice salad 117
49. Pinto Bean, Rice, and Veggie Salad 119
50. Edamame And Pinto Bean Salad 121
51. Rice & bean salad with minced crudite 123
52. Bean and Rice Soup 125
53. Chili con Carne 127
54. Vegan Rice Soup 129
55. Bean and rice burritos 131
56. Rice and Bean Roll-Ups 133
57. Baked Pinto Bean Flautas with rice flour Tortilla 135
58. Bean and rice burgers 138
59. Rice and bean enchiladas with red sauce 140
60. Rice And Bean Quesadillas 143
61. Peruvian Tacu Tacu Cake 145
62. Alkaline Stew Peas with Dumplings 148
63. Bean and rice pudding with raisins and nuts 151

CRAWFISH ÉTOUFFÉE 153
   64. Shrimp Étouffée 154
   65. Crawfish Étouffée 156

GRITS 158
   66. Grits and Grillades 159
   67. Shrimp and Grits 161
   68. Shrimp, Andouille Sausage, and Grits 163
   69. Creamy Cheesy Grits 165
   70. Hominy souffle 167

71. Goat cheese polenta with sun dried tomatoes 169
FRIED CATFISH 171
72. Classic Southern Fried Catfish 172
73. Cajun Blackened Catfish 174
74. Cornmeal-Crusted Fried Catfish 176
75. Panko-Crusted Fried Catfish 178
76. Lemon-Pepper Fried Catfish 180
77. Buttermilk and Hot Sauce Fried Catfish 182
BOUDIN BALLS 184
78. Classic Boudin Balls 185
79. Spicy Boudin Balls 187
80. Cheese-Stuffed Boudin Balls 189
81. Crawfish Boudin Balls 191
82. Smoked Boudin Balls 193
PO' BOYS 195
83. Shrimp Po' Boy 196
84. Oyster Po' Boy 198
85. Fried Chicken Po' Boy 200
86. Catfish Po' Boy 202
87. Roast Beef Po' Boy 204
REDFISH COURTBOUILLON 206
88. Louisiana Redfish Courtbouillon 207
89. Emeril Lagasse Redfish Courtbouillon 209
90. Saveur Redfish Courtbouillon 211
BEIGNETS 213
91. Grand Marnier beignets 214
92. Beignets with cinnamon sugar 217
LAGNIAPPE 220
93. Lagniappe 221
94. Calas 224
95. Corn Maque Choux 226
96. Crawfish Bisque 228
97. Crawfish Étouffée 231
98. Crawfish Pies 233
99. Dirty Rice 236
100. Eggs Sardou 238
CONCLUSION 241

INTRODUCTION

Cajun cuisine is known for its bold and spicy flavors, influenced by the diverse cultures that have shaped Louisiana's culinary traditions. From seafood gumbo to jambalaya, crawfish etouffee to blackened catfish, Cajun cuisine has something for everyone.

In this cookbook, we're excited to share 100 authentic and delicious Cajun recipes that are sure to spice up your kitchen. Whether you're a seasoned pro or a newcomer to this flavorful cuisine, we've got you covered. Our recipes are easy to follow, with step-by-step instructions and helpful tips to ensure that your dishes turn out perfectly every time. We'll also be sharing some background information on Cajun cuisine and its history, as well as tips for mastering the unique flavors and techniques that make this cuisine so special.

So, join us on this journey to discover the art of Cajun cooking. With our 100 recipes, you'll be able to bring the flavors of Louisiana into your own kitchen and impress your friends and family with your culinary skills.

In this cookbook, you'll find:

I. Authentic Cajun ingredients and spices
II. Seafood and meat dishes
III. Delicious vegetarian options
IV. Easy-to-follow recipes for classic dishes
V. Unique twists on traditional favorites
VI. Tips for perfecting the Cajun cooking techniques
VII. Information on Cajun culture and history
VIII. Mouth-watering photos of every dish

And so much more! So, whether you're looking to impress your dinner guests or simply enjoy some spicy and flavorful meals, this cookbook is for you.

GUMBO

1. Jamaican Squash Soup

MAKES 4

INGREDIENTS:
- 1 large onion, peeled and chopped
- 1 carrot, peeled and chopped
- 1 jalapeño, pepper, seeds removed, finely chopped
- 3 tablespoons butter
- 2 teaspoon ground cumin
- 2 teaspoon ground coriander
- ½ teaspoon ground cinnamon
- ½ teaspoon cayenne pepper
- ½ teaspoon chili powder
- 1 large spaghetti squash, peeled and diced
- Chicken stock to cover vegetables, about 3 cups
- Juice of 1 orange
- Juice of 1 lime

ANCHO CREAM
- 2 to 3 Ancho chilies, halved, stemmed, and seeded
- 6 tablespoons almond milk
- 4 tablespoons sour cream
- Salt
- Pepper
- Lime juice to taste

INSTRUCTIONS:
a) In a large heavy pot, sweat onion, carrot, and Jalapeno pepper in butter until soft
b) Add cumin, coriander, cinnamon, cayenne, and chili powder
c) Cook for additional 2 minutes over low heat
d) Add squash
e) Cover mixture with stock, juice of one orange, and juice of a lime Simmer until squash is soft, about ½ hour
f) Allow cooling
g) Purée mixture in processor or use immersion blender
h) Return soup to the pan, season with salt and pepper
i) Reheat and adjust seasoning if necessary
j) Swirl in Ancho Cream
k) Garnish with sour cream thinned with some heavy cream
l) Place dab in the center of a soup bowl and using a toothpick, drag from center to outside and form a star or spider web

2. Keto egg drop soup

MAKES: 1

INGREDIENTS:
a) 1 ½ cups Chicken Broth
b) ½ cube Chicken Bouillon
c) 1 tablespoons Butter
d) 2 large Eggs
e) 1 teaspoon Chilli Garlic Paste

INSTRUCTIONS:
a) Place a pan on the stovetop and turn it to medium-high heat.
b) Add the chicken broth, bouillon cube, and butter. Bring to a boil.
c) Stir in the chili garlic paste.
d) Beat the eggs separately and add them to the simmering broth.
e) Combine thoroughly and cook for 3 more minutes.
f) Serve.

3. Jamaican shrimp soup

MAKES: 2

INGREDIENTS:
- 2 tablespoons Green Curry Paste
- 1 cup Vegetable Stock
- 1 cup Coconut Milk
- 6 oz. Precooked Shrimp
- 5 oz. Broccoli Florets
- 3 tablespoons Cilantro, chopped
- 2 tablespoons Coconut Oil
- 1 tablespoon Soy Sauce
- Juice of ½ Lime
- 1 medium Spring Onion, chopped
- 1 teaspoon Crushed Roasted Garlic
- 1 teaspoon Minced Ginger
- 1 teaspoon Fish Sauce
- ½ teaspoon Turmeric
- ½ cup Sour Cream

INSTRUCTIONS:
a) In a medium-sized saucepan, melt the coconut oil.
b) Add the garlic, ginger, spring onions, green curry paste, and turmeric. Add the soy sauce, and fish sauce.
c) Cook for 2 minutes.
d) Add vegetable stock and coconut milk and stir thoroughly. Cook for a few minutes on low heat.
e) Add the broccoli florets and cilantro and stir thoroughly once the curry has thickened a little.
f) When you're satisfied with the curry's consistency, add the shrimp and lime juice, and stir everything together.
g) Cook for a few minutes on low heat. If necessary, season with salt and pepper.

4. Stewed Calaloo

INGREDIENTS:
- Chopped calaloo leaves
- 3 tablespoons of vegetable oil
- 2 minced garlic cloves
- 2 medium onions
- 1 cup Coconut milk
- Salt
- Pepper
- Hot pepper sauce

INSTRUCTIONS:

a) Heat oil in a heavy saucepan. Add chopped onions and garlic. When soft, add calaloo leaves and toss until coated with oil and wilted.

b) Add coconut milk until enough to cover calaloo. Simmer until the calaloo is soft and most of the milk has evaporated.

c) Add seasonings and serve as a vegetable.

5. Coconut Prawn Soup

MAKES: 4

INGREDIENTS:
- 600g of raw prawns, deveined
- 1 small onion chopped
- 2 medium-sized carrots chopped
- 1 red bell pepper chopped
- 2-3 cups of spinach or kale, chopped
- 2 scallion chopped
- a handful of whole okra
- 4 garlic cloves minced
- 1 tablespoon ginger minced
- 1 can of coconut milk
- 1 liter of vegetable stock
- 1 teaspoon of seafood seasoning
- 1 teaspoon of black pepper
- 5 sprigs of fresh thyme
- 2 teaspoons of parsley
- 1 scotch bonnet
- ¼ teaspoon of red chili flakes for heat
- a squeeze of fresh lime juice
- ⅛ teaspoon of Himalayan pink salt
- coconut oil
- 1 tablespoon of tapioca mixed with 2 tablespoons of warm water for a thicker soup

INSTRUCTIONS:
a) Place the prawns into a medium bowl and marinate with the seafood seasoning, then set aside.
b) Melt 2 tablespoons of coconut oil in a large saucepan on medium heat.
c) Proceed to add the onions, scallion, and garlic then sauté until soft and translucent.
d) Add the carrots, garlic, bell peppers, and spinach and continue to cook for 5 minutes

e) Add the black pepper, parsley, thyme, and chili flakes (if using) and stir and combine with the veggies.

f) Pour the vegetable stock and coconut milk into the saucepan then bring to a rolling boil

g) Add the scotch bonnet and then reduce the heat to low with the lid on.

h) Simmer for 20 minutes

i) After 15 minutes, add the okra and prawns and stir in the tapioca paste if you want the soup to be slightly thicker

j) Squeeze the lime over the entire soup and leave to simmer for another 5 minutes.

6. Gungo Pea Soup

MAKES 6-8

INGREDIENTS:
- 2 cups (400 g) dried gungo or pigeon peas
- 1 smoked ham hock
- 2 medium onions, cut into large pieces
- 2 carrots, cut into large pieces
- 1 stalk celery, with leaves
- 2 scotch bonnet or jalapeño chilies, deseeded and diced
- 1 clove of garlic, minced
- 1 bay leaf
- 1 teaspoon crushed fresh rosemary leaves or ¼ teaspoon crushed dried rosemary
- 1 portion Spinners

INSTRUCTIONS:
a) Prepare the Spinners
b) Wash the peas and place them in a bowl. Add enough water to cover and soak overnight. Drain and set aside.
c) Add 6 cups of water to a stockpot and add the ham hock, onions, carrots, celery, chilies, garlic, bay leaf, and rosemary. Bring to a boil, reduce the heat to low, and simmer for 45 minutes. Strain the stock, reserving the ham hock and discarding the vegetables. Skim the fat from the stock.
d) Return the stock and the ham hock to the stockpot along with the soaked peas. Simmer over low heat until the peas are tender, about 2 hours. Remove half of the peas from the soup with a slotted spoon and purée in a food processor.
e) Return the purée to the soup.
f) Add the prepared Spinners to the soup and heat through.

7. Instant Pot Lentil Gumbo

Makes: 6

INGREDIENTS:
- 1 cup cauliflower, finely chopped
- 1 can salt-free tomatoes, diced
- 1 cup lentils
- 2 tablespoons Apple Cider vinegar
- 1 ½ cup chopped onion
- 2 cups fresh okra, chopped
- 2 tablespoons vegetable broth
- 1 teaspoon Cajun mix spice
- 1 red bell pepper, chopped
- ½ cup tomato sauce
- 1 teaspoon minced garlic
- 3 cups vegetable broth
- 2 celery ribs, chopped
- ½ tablespoon fresh oregano
- 1 tablespoon fresh thyme
- ½ teaspoon cayenne
- Kosher salt to taste
- Sliced jalapeno and fresh cilantro to garnish
- Slurry to thicken

INSTRUCTIONS:

a) In a pot, sauté the vegetable broth, onion, garlic, bell pepper, and celery for 5 minutes until softened and aromatic.

b) Add the spices and mix again for 1 minute.

c) Add remaining ingredients except for salt and pepper, then mix.

d) Place the lid on a pressure cooker then set it to cook for at least 12 minutes. The natural release works best to make sure the lentils are fully cooked. But if you're in a bind, cover the vent with a cloth, then quick release.

e) After cooking, add ½ teaspoon of salt and pepper. Stir and keep it warm for 10 minutes until the gumbo has a thick consistency. (Don't add extra salt while cooking the gumbo).

f) Prepare to serve in bowls and garnish with jalapeños, fresh cilantro, and red pepper flakes.

8. Alaska octopus gumbo

Makes: 4 Servings

INGREDIENTS:
½ cup Diced bacon
2 cups Water
1 pint Fresh octopus, steamed until tender
2 cups Slightly undercooked steamed rice
1 pounds Canned tomatoes
1 Can okra
½ cup Diced onions
1 Diced green pepper
¼ teaspoon Cayenne
½ cup Diced celery
Salt and pepper to taste

Boil bacon in water for 15 minutes, then add the rest of the ingredients . Simmer together for ten minutes. Serve with warm cornbread.

9. Baked vegetable gumbo creole

Makes: 10 servings

INGREDIENTS:
1 pounds Fresh okra,diag. sliced
2 packs Frozen sliced okra(10oz)
Boiling salted water
1 Rib celery,diagonally sliced
2 Bell peppers,in strips
2 packs Frozen lima beans(10oz)
8 Ears fresh corn kernels
2 packs Frozen corn,thawed(10oz)
Butter or margarine
Bread crumbs
1 Small onion,chopped
4 Ripe tomatoes,sliced
2 Serrano chiles,thinly sliced
1 teaspoon Chopped fresh basil
½ teaspoon Dried basil,crumbled
Salt to taste
Black pepper to taste
½ cup Shredded Monterey Jack

INSTRUCTIONS:
a) Cook fresh okra briefly in boiling salted water; drain.
b) Blanch celery in boiling salted water.
c) Add bell peppers and lima beans and cook until just tender; during last 30 seconds, add corn (do not overcook), then drain vegetables.
d) Butter a large baking dish and sprinkle with bread crumbs; add a layer of corn-bean mixture and okra.
e) Combine onion, tomatoes and basil; spoon layer of onion-tomato mixture over bottom layer in dish.
f) Sprinkle with chiles and season with salt and pepper.
g) Dot with butter and sprinkle with bread crumbs.
h) Repeat layering until casserole is filled.
i) Top with a layer of okra that has been dipped in crumbs and lightly sauteed in butter; sprinkle evenly with shredded cheese if desired.
j) Bake uncovered in preheated 300' over for 1 hour.

10. Cajun catfish gumbo

Makes: 10 Servings

INGREDIENTS:
2 cups Chopped onions
2 cups Green onions; chopped *
1 cup Chopped celery
½ cup Bell pepper; chopped
6 Cl Garlic; chopped
6 7-oz catfish fillets; cut in
3 7-oz catfish fillets; for st
1 pounds Crab meat; (claw)
1 pounds Shrimp; (peeled)
1½ cup Oil
1½ cup Flour
4 quarts Hot water
Salt; to taste
Cayenne pepper; to taste
* separate and reserve greens.

INSTRUCTIONS:
a) In separate pot, simmer 3 (7 oz.) catfish fillets in 1 quart of lightly salted water for 15 minutes. Strain through cheese cloth and reserve liquid. Chop catfish and reserve meat. In heavy bottom gumbo pot, add oil and flour. Cook over medium high heat stirring constantly until golden brown. Caution, do not scorch! Add all seasonings except green onions tops. Saute for 5 minutes.

b) Add all fish stock and chopped catfish. Add hot water, one ladle at a time, until consistency of thick soup is achieved. Add claw crab meat, and half of shrimp. Reduce to simmer. Cook approximately 45 minutes, stirring occasionally. Add catfish, remaining shrimp and green onions tops. Cook 10-15 minutes. Season to taste using salt and cayenne pepper. Add water if necessary to retain volume. Serve over white rice.

JAMBALAYA

11. Slow Cooker Jambalaya

MAKES 6–8 SERVINGS

INGREDIENTS:
- 1 ½ pounds boneless chicken thighs, rinsed, trimmed of excess fat, and cut into 1-inch cubes
- 3 links Cajun smoked sausage (about 14 ounces total), cut into 1/4-inch-thick rounds
- 1 medium onion, chopped
- 1 green bell pepper, chopped
- 1 celery stalk, chopped
- 3 garlic cloves, minced
- 2 tablespoons tomato paste
- 1 teaspoon Creole seasoning
- 1 teaspoon salt
- ½ teaspoon freshly ground black pepper
- ½ teaspoon Tabasco sauce
- ½ teaspoon Worcestershire sauce
- 2 cups chicken broth
- 1 ½ cups long-grain rice
- 2 pounds medium shrimp, peeled and deveined (optional)

INSTRUCTIONS:
a) Place all the ingredients (except the shrimp, if using) into a slow cooker. Stir together, cover, and cook on low for 5 hours.
b) If using shrimp, gently stir them in after the 5 hours of cooking and cook on high for 30 minutes to 1 hour more, or until the shrimp are done but not overcooked.

12. Red Bean Jambalaya

Makes 4 servings

INGREDIENTS:
- 1 tablespoon olive oil
- 1 medium yellow onion, chopped
- 2 celery ribs, chopped
- 1 medium green bell pepper, chopped
- 3 garlic cloves, minced
- 1 cup long-grain rice
- 3 cups cooked or 2 (15.5-ounce) cans dark red kidney beans
- 1 (14.5-ounce) can diced tomatoes, drained
- (14.5-ounce) can crushed tomatoes
- (4-ounce) can mild green chiles, drained
- 1 teaspoon dried thyme
- 1/2 teaspoon dried marjoram
- 1 teaspoon salt
- Freshly ground black pepper
- 2 1/2 cups vegetable broth
- 1 tablespoon chopped fresh parsley, for garnish
- Tabasco sauce (optional)

INSTRUCTIONS:
a) In a large saucepan, heat the oil over medium heat. Add the onion, celery, bell pepper, and garlic. Cover and cook until softened, about 7 minutes.

b) Stir in the rice, beans, diced tomatoes, crushed tomatoes, chiles, thyme, marjoram, salt, and black pepper to taste. Add the broth, cover, and simmer until the vegetables are soft and the rice is tender, about 45 minutes.

c) Sprinkle with parsley and a splash of Tabasco, if using, and serve.

13. Baked Jambalaya Casserole

Makes 4 servings

INGREDIENTS:
- 10 ounces tempeh
- 2 tablespoons olive oil
- 1 medium yellow onion, chopped
- 1 medium green bell pepper, chopped
- 2 garlic cloves, minced
- 1 (28-ounce) can diced tomatoes, undrained
- 1/2 cup white rice
- 1 1/2 cups vegetable broth
- 1 1/2 cups cooked or 1 (15.5-ounce) can dark red kidney beans
- 1 tablespoon chopped fresh parsley
- 1 1/2 teaspoons Cajun seasoning
- 1 teaspoon dried thyme
- 1/2 teaspoon salt
- 1/4 teaspoon freshly ground black pepper

INSTRUCTIONS:
a) In a medium saucepan of simmering water, cook the tempeh for 30 minutes. Drain and pat dry. Cut into 1/2-inch dice. Preheat the oven to 350°F.
b) In a large skillet, heat 1 tablespoon of the oil over medium heat. Add the tempeh and cook until browned on both sides, about 8 minutes. Transfer the tempeh to a 9 x 13-inch baking dish and set aside.
c) In the same skillet, heat the remaining 1 tablespoon oil over medium heat. Add the onion, bell pepper, and garlic. Cover and cook until the vegetables are softened, about 7 minutes.
d) Add the vegetable mixture to the baking dish with the tempeh. Stir in the tomatoes with their liquid, the rice, broth, kidney beans, parsley, Cajun seasoning, thyme, salt, and black pepper.
e) Mix well, then cover tightly and bake until the rice is tender, about 1 hour. Serve immediately.

14. Sausage Jambalaya

Makes: 6–8 servings

INGREDIENTS:
- ½ cup butter or margarine
- 1 large onion, chopped
- 1 large green bell pepper, chopped
- ½ cup diced celery
- 1 tablespoon minced garlic
- 1 pound fully cooked smoked sausage links, sliced
- 3 cups chicken broth
- 2 cups uncooked white rice
- 1 cup chopped tomatoes
- ½ cup chopped green onion
- 1-½ tablespoons parsley
- 1 tablespoon Worcestershire sauce
- 1 tablespoon Tabasco sauce

INSTRUCTIONS:
- Preheat oven to 375 degrees.
- In a frying pan, melt butter. Sauté onion, bell pepper, celery, and garlic in butter until tender.
- In a large bowl, combine sausage, broth, rice, tomatoes, green onion, parsley, Worcestershire sauce, and Tabasco sauce. Stir sautéed vegetables into sausage mixture.
- Spread into a greased 9x13-inch pan.
- Cover and bake 20 minutes. Stir, cover, and bake 20 minutes more.
- Stir, cover, and bake a final 5–10 minutes, or until rice is done.

15. Chicken Jambalaya with Sausage

Makes 1 quart

- 1 tablespoon olive oil
- 3 to 4-pounds (1.4 to 1.8-kg) boneless, skinless chicken thighs and breasts, cut into bite-sized pieces
- 2 cups smoked sausage, cut into chunks
- 2 cups chopped onion
- 2 cups chopped bell pepper
- 2 ribs celery, chopped
- 6 cloves garlic, minced
- 2 tablespoons smoked paprika
- 2 tablespoons dried thyme
- Cayenne pepper, to taste
- 2 tablespoons Cajun spice blend
- 6 cups peeled tomatoes with juice, divided
- ¼ teaspoon hot pepper sauce
- 4 cups chicken broth
- 4 cups water
- Salt and pepper, to taste

a) In a large stockpot, warm the olive oil and lightly brown the first 6 **INGREDIENTS:**.
b) In a small bowl, mix paprika, salt, pepper, thyme, cayenne, and Cajun spice blend.
c) Sprinkle the vegetable and meat mixture with spice mixture, then add tomatoes and hot sauce, and stir well to combine.
d) Ladle the ingredients into sanitized quart jars, filling them no more than halfway.
e) Meanwhile, place the broth, tomato juice, and water in the stockpot and bring it to a boil, deglazing the bottom of the pot.
f) Ladle 2 cups of hot liquid into each jar, allowing 1 inch of headspace. You can top up with water if you need to.
g) Lid the jars and process in a pressure canner for 90 minutes at 10 PSI, adjusting for altitude.

16. Jambalaya-Stuffed Cabbage Rolls

Makes: 6 TO 8 SERVINGS

INGREDIENTS:
- 2 tablespoons extra-virgin olive oil
- 1 pound andouille sausage, chopped
- 1 large red bell pepper, diced
- 1 large green bell pepper, diced
- 1 large red onion, chopped
- 1 (14.5-ounce) can diced tomatoes, undrained
- 2 tablespoons tomato paste
- 5 garlic cloves, minced
- 2½ teaspoons Cajun seasoning, divided
- 2 teaspoons dried thyme
- 2 teaspoons paprika
- 2 teaspoons Worcestershire sauce
- 1½ teaspoons celery salt
- 3 bay leaves
- 6 cups vegetable broth, divided
- 1½ cups uncooked white rice
- 1 pound medium raw shrimp, peeled and deveined
- 1 large head of cabbage, leaves individually removed
- Vegetable oil, for greasing
- 1 cup canned tomato sauce
- Kosher salt and black pepper, to taste

INSTRUCTIONS:
a) In a large stockpot over medium heat, drizzle the oil. Once the oil is hot, toss in the sausage and cook until it browns. Remove the sausage from the pot and set it to the side.

b) Next, add the peppers and onions. Cook until they are nice and tender, then add in the tomatoes (with the juice), tomato paste, and garlic. Stir well. Add in 2 teaspoons of the Cajun seasoning, the thyme, paprika, Worcestershire sauce, celery salt, bay leaves, and 3 cups of the vegetable broth. Stir the ingredients , then add the sausage back into the pot, along with the uncooked rice. Stir again

and cook for 25 to 30 minutes, or until the liquid is absorbed. Then add the shrimp, stir, and remove from the heat. Set to the side.
c) In a separate stockpot over medium heat, add the cabbage leaves and the remaining 3 cups vegetable broth. Cook until the cabbage softens, then drain and cool.
d) Lightly oil a baking dish. Wrap about ¼ cup jambalaya in each cabbage leaf and place the rolls in the baking dish. Set to the side.
e) In a small bowl, combine the tomato sauce, the remaining ½ teaspoon Cajun seasoning, salt, and pepper. Stir until well combined.
f) Pour the tomato sauce all over the cabbage rolls, then cover the baking dish with aluminum foil and bake in the oven for 25 to 30 minutes. Remove from the oven and let cool before serving.

17. Quinoa jambalaya

Makes: 6 Servings

INGREDIENTS:
- 1 tablespoon Hot Pepper Sesame Oil
- 1 tablespoon whole wheat flour
- 1 medium Onion; diced
- 1 Garlic clove; minced
- 28 ounces Crushed Tomatoes
- 1 Bay leaf
- ½ tablespoon Dried thyme
- ¾ teaspoon Lima sea salt
- 1 cup Eden Quinoa; rinsed
- 1 Green pepper; diced
- ½ cup Parsley, chopped
- 1 cup Celery; chopped
- 2 Green onions; thinly sliced

INSTRUCTIONS:
a) Heat oil in a heavy saucepan. Add flour and stir until a fragrant aroma is released (3 minutes). Add onion, garlic, tomatoes, bay leaf, thyme and salt. Mix and simmer, covered for 10 minutes.

b) Add water to stock. Bring to boil. Add quinoa, green pepper, parsley, celery, and green onion. Cover and cook another 3-5 minutes longer.

c) Turn heat off and let sit covered for 10 minutes. Add pepper. Mix well. Serve.

18. Alligator jambalaya

Makes: 256 Inch links

INGREDIENTS:
- 1 pounds Marinated alligator fillet cut into small pieces
- 1 pounds Hot sausage (italian) cut into chunks
- 3 tablespoons Oil
- ⅔ cup Bell peppers chopped
- 2 cloves Garlic crushed
- ¾ cup Parsley
- 1 cup Chopped fresh parsley
- 1 cup Chopped celery
- 2 cans Tomatoes (16 oz each)
- 2 cups Chicken stock
- 1 cup Green onion
- 2 teaspoons Oregano
- 2 dashes Red hot sauce (optional)
- Cajun spices
- Salt to taste
- 2 cups Raw white rice

a) Saute the bell pepper, garlic, parsley and celery. While this is cooking, add tomatoes & their liquid, the chicken stock &, green onion to a pot that can cook on the stove and in the oven (Corning ware)

b) Stir in spices, sauteed vegetables raw rice, sausage and alligator fillet pieces.

c) Cook on medium-high heat until liquid is absorbed and then bake covered in the oven for 25 minutes.

19. Bayou boeuf jambalaya

Makes: 6 servings

INGREDIENTS:
1 tablespoon Shortening
¼ pounds Kosher salami, cubed
1 Sprig thyme
1 Onion, sliced
Salt & Pepper to taste
2 cups Tomatoes
1 cup Uncooked long grain rice
1 tablespoon Flour
¼ cup Green pepper, minced
1 Bay leaf
1 Sprig parsley, minced
1 Clove garlic, minced
1 pounds Kosher smoked sausage.
1¼ cup Tomato juice

Melt shortening in heavy saucepan over medium heat. Stir in flour, salami, and green pepper. Simmer 5 min, stirring constantly.

Add remaining ingredients except rice. Bring to boil. Add rice to liquid. Cover and simmer for 40 min. until all liquid is absorbed.

20. Black-eyed peas and sausage jambalaya

Makes: 25 Servings

INGREDIENTS:
2 pounds White onions; chopped
2 bunches Green onion; chopped
1 large Green bell pepper; chopped
5 Cloves garlic; chopped
1 cup Parsley; chopped
3 pounds Salt meat*
3 pounds Smoked hot sausage
3 pounds Uncooked rice
12 cups Water

*boiled once, cut in small pieces Fry sausage and cut into bite-size pieces. Saute onion, pepper, garlic and parsley. Cook until limp. Add salt meat, sausage, blackeyed peas, and rice.

Season to taste. Add 12 cups water. Bring to a boil; mix well and cover tightly. Cook on lowest heat for 45 minutes. Do not remove cover during this time. Remove cover for 5 to 10 minutes before serving.

RED BEANS AND RICE

21. Long-grain Rice and pinto bean

Servings: 4

INGREDIENTS
- 50ml/2fl oz vegetable oil
- 1 onion, finely chopped
- 300ml/10½ oz. long-grain rice
- 400ml/14½ oz. water
- 400ml/14½ oz. coconut milk
- 400g/14¼oz tin pinto beans, rinsed and drained
- 3 tablespoons fresh thyme
- salt and freshly ground black pepper
- fresh coriander, to garnish

DIRECTIONS

a) Heat the oil in a frying pan and fry the onion until translucent.
b) Add the rice, stir well and add the water and coconut milk. Bring to the boil.
c) Add the pinto beans and thyme, simmer, and cover, for about 20 minutes until the rice is cooked. Season with salt and freshly ground black pepper.
d) Serve garnished with the coriander.

22. Lime chicken with egg-fried long-grain rice

Servings: 2

INGREDIENTS
For The Chicken
- 2 skinless chicken breasts
- 2 tablespoon sesame oil
- 2 teaspoon vegetable oil
- 2 tablespoon soy sauce
- 2 garlic cloves, finely chopped
- ½ lemon, grated zest, and juice
- salt and freshly ground black pepper
- 1 tablespoon clear honey

For The Rice
- 2 tablespoon groundnut oil
- 2-3 teaspoon sesame oil
- 2 free-range eggs, lightly beaten
- splash soy sauce
- 2 spring onions, finely chopped
- 50g/2oz pinto beans, cooked
- 150g/5oz long-grain rice, cooked
- salt and freshly ground black pepper
- 3-4 tablespoons chopped coriander
- lime wedges, to serve

DIRECTIONS

a) To butterfly, the chicken breasts lay them on a board and use a sharp knife to make a cut parallel to the chopping board three-quarters of the way through each breast.

b) Open each chicken breast out so you have two large, thinner chicken breasts.

c) Place them in a bowl with one tablespoon of the sesame oil, the vegetable oil, soy sauce, garlic, lemon zest, and juice.

d) Season with salt and freshly ground black pepper and mix to combine. In a separate bowl, mix the honey with the remaining sesame oil.

e) Heat a griddle pan over medium-high heat until smoking then lay the chicken on the griddle and cook for 2-3 minutes on each side, brushing it once or twice with the honey and sesame mixture.
f) When it's done the chicken should be char-grilled on the outside and completely cooked through. Leave to rest for 2-3 minutes.
g) Meanwhile, for the rice, heat a wok over high heat then add the groundnut and one teaspoon of the sesame oil. When the oil starts to shimmer add the eggs and cook, stirring all the time, for 1-2 minutes or until they're scrambled.
h) Push the eggs to the side of the pan and add a little more sesame oil, the soy sauce, spring onions, and pinto beans and cook for one minute then add the rice and season with salt and freshly ground black pepper.
i) Cook, stirring continuously, for 3-4 minutes, or until warmed through. Stir through the coriander.
j) To serve, spoon the rice onto plates. Cut the chicken on the diagonal into thin strips and place it on top of the rice. Top with a wedge of lime.

23. Long-grain Rice Hoppin' John

Servings: 4

INGREDIENTS
- 2 tablespoon vegetable oil
- 300g/10½oz cooked and shredded bacon
- 1 green pepper, finely chopped
- 1 red pepper, finely chopped
- 1 red onion, finely chopped
- 3 celery sticks, finely chopped
- 4 garlic cloves, crushed
- 1 teaspoon dried chili flakes
- 2 bay leaves
- 1 litre/1¾ pint of chicken or vegetable stock
- 400g/14oz tin pinto beans, drained and rinsed
- 225g/8oz long-grain rice
- 2 tablespoon Creole or all-purpose seasoning
- salt and freshly ground black pepper
- To serve
- a handful of flat-leaf parsley leaves, finely chopped
- bunch spring onions, finely chopped

DIRECTIONS

a) Heat the oil in a large pan over medium heat.
b) Add bacon to the pan and fry until crispy. Remove with a slotted spoon and drain on kitchen paper.
c) Add the onion, peppers, celery, garlic, chili flakes, bay leaves, Creole seasoning, salt, and pepper to the pan and sauté on a low to medium heat until softened.
d) Pour in the stock and bring to a boil.
e) Add the rice, beans, and bacon, and stir well. Cover and simmer for 20 minutes, or until the rice is tender and most of the liquid has been absorbed.
f) Divide between serving bowls, sprinkle with the parsley and spring onions and serve.

24. Mexican-Inspired Pinto Beans and Rice

Servings:: 8

INGREDIENTS
- 1 tablespoon Chicken Bouillon (Reduced Sodium)
- 3 tablespoons tomato paste
- 1 teaspoon ground coriander seeds
- 1 teaspoons salt
- ½ teaspoons garlic powder
- ¼ teaspoons pepper
- 3½ cups water
- 2 cups long-grain white rice, rinsed using a mesh strainer
- 1 red bell pepper, stemmed, seeded, and diced
- ¼ cup finely chopped red onion
- 1 jalapeño, stemmed, seeded, and finely diced
- 2 tablespoons finely chopped cilantro
- 1 can (15-ounce) pinto beans, drained and rinsed

DIRECTIONS

a) To a pot, add Chicken Base, tomato paste, coriander, salt, garlic powder, and pepper; whisk to combine.
b) Gradually whisk in water, add rice and stir to combine. Place a pot over medium-high heat and bring to a boil, stirring occasionally.
c) Reduce heat to medium-low, cover. Continue to cook until liquid has been absorbed, stirring occasionally, about 12-15 minutes. Remove from heat and let stand covered for a few minutes.
d) Place rice in a large bowl and add bell pepper, onion, jalapeño, and cilantro; stir to combine.
e) Gently stir in beans and serve.

25. Pinto Beans and Rice with Cilantro

Servings 6
INGREDIENTS
For the Rice:
- 1 cup long-grain white rice
- 1 tablespoon olive oil
- 8 oz can of tomato sauce
- 1 red bell pepper cored, seeded, and quartered
- 1 1/2 cups chicken stock or vegetable broth
- 3/4 teaspoon kosher salt
- 1 teaspoon garlic powder
- 1/4 teaspoon chili powder
- 1/4 teaspoon cumin
- 1/2 cup diced tomatoes
- 2 tablespoons chopped cilantro for garnish optional

For the Beans:
- 15 ounce can of pinto beans drained and rinsed
- 1/2 cup chicken stock or vegetable broth
- 1 tablespoon tomato paste
- 3/4 teaspoon salt
- 3/4 teaspoon chili powder
- 1/2 cup pico de gallo for garnish optional

DIRECTIONS
For the Rice:
a) Heat the olive oil in a 2-quart pot over medium heat. Add the rice and stir until the rice is coated in the oil. Cook for about 5 minutes or until the rice is toasted and lightly browned.
b) Add all of the remaining ingredients.
c) Return the pot to the burner, and bring the contents to a boil.
d) Cover the pot and turn the heat to low; cook for 17 minutes.
e) Take the pot off the heat and let it stand, covered for 5 minutes. Remove and discard bell peppers. Stir well. Garnish with tomatoes and green onions if desired.

For the Beans:
f) Put all of the ingredients in a pan over medium-high heat, and bring to a simmer. Cook for 7-10 minutes until the sauce has thickened. Taste and add more salt or chili powder if needed. You can also add a bit more chicken stock if the sauce gets too thick for your liking. Garnish with pico de gallo if desired.

26. Spanish Pinto Beans & Rice

Servings 2

INGREDIENTS
FOR THE RICE
- 2 cups vegetable broth 475 ml
- 1 cup long-grain rice 190 grams
- 1/4 teaspoons saffron threads .17 grams
- pinch sea salt
- dash black pepper

FOR THE BEANS
- 2 tablespoons extra virgin olive oil 30 ml
- 1 small onion
- 4 cloves garlic
- 1 carrot
- 1 green bell pepper
- 1 teaspoon sweet smoked Spanish paprika 2.30 grams
- 1/2 teaspoon ground cumin 1.25 grams
- 2 1/2 cups canned pinto beans 400 grams
- 1 cup vegetable broth 240 ml
- pinch sea salt
- dash black pepper
- a handful of finely chopped fresh parsley

DIRECTIONS

a) Add 2 cups vegetable broth into a saucepan, pinch in 1/4 teaspoons saffron threads, and season with sea salt & freshly cracked black pepper, heat with a high heat

b) Meanwhile, add 1 cup of long-grain rice into a sieve and rinse under cold running water, until the water runs clear underneath the sieve

c) Once the broth comes to a boil, add the rice into the pan, give it a mix and place a lid on the pan, lower to low-medium heat, and simmer until the rice is cooked.

d) Meanwhile, heat a large fry-pan with medium heat and add 2 tablespoons extra virgin olive oil, after 2 minutes add 1 small onion finely diced, 1 green bell pepper finely chopped, 1 carrot

e) (peeled) finely chopped, and 4 cloves garlic roughly minced, mix the vegetable continuously with the olive oil
e) After 4 minutes and the vegetables are lightly sautéed, add in 1 teaspoon sweet smoked Spanish paprika and 1/2 teaspoons ground cumin, quickly mix, then add in 2 1/2 cups canned pinto beans (drained & rinsed) and season with sea salt & black pepper, gently mix until well mixed, then add in 1 cup vegetable broth and simmer on a medium heat
f) Once the rice is cooked through (15 minutes in my case), remove the rice from the heat, let it sit for 3 to 4 minutes with the lid on, then remove the lid and fluff up the rice with a fork, transfer the rice into serving dishes
g) Grab the simmering beans (there should still be a little broth left) and add them into the serving dish next to the rice, sprinkle with freshly chopped parsley, and enjoy!

27. One-Pot Rice and Beans

Total Time: 30 minutes

INGREDIENTS
- 2 tablespoons olive oil
- 1 yellow onion, chopped (about 1 ¼ cups)
- 1 ¾ cups chicken or vegetable stock or water
- 1 teaspoon salt
- 1 cup long-grain rice
- 1 (15.5-ounce) can of black or pinto beans
- Lime wedges or cilantro leaves, for garnish (optional)

DIRECTIONS

h) In a large saucepan or Dutch oven with a tight-fitting lid, warm the olive oil over medium heat. Add onion and sauté until translucent, about 3 minutes. Add the stock, cover, and bring to a boil.

i) Add the salt, rice, and beans (including the liquid). Stir just to combine, then cover.

j) Turn the heat down as low as it will go, then let simmer, undisturbed, for 18 to 20 minutes. Remove from heat and let sit for 4 minutes, then fluff with a fork.

k) Season to taste with salt and pepper, then garnish with lime or cilantro as you wish.

28. Southern Pinto Beans and Rice

Servings: 6 cups

INGREDIENTS
- 1 lb. dried pinto beans
- 8 cups water or broth
- 2 tablespoons salt, for overnight soaking; table salt
- 2 tablespoons onion powder or 1 cup fresh, diced onion
- 2 tablespoons garlic powder
- 2 cups rice, brown or white rice, cooked
- 1 smoked ham hock
- salt and pepper to taste

DIRECTIONS
a) Put beans in a large Dutch oven with onion and garlic powder, liquid, and protein (optional).
b) Cook on low heat, uncovered, for 3-4 hours or until tender; check liquid level frequently; add more if needed; when tender, taste for seasonings and adjust accordingly
c) 1 lb. dried pinto beans,8 cups water or broth,2 tablespoons onion powder,2 tablespoons garlic powder,1 smoked ham hock

29. Pinto Beans and Rice and Sausage

Servings: 6 servings

INGREDIENTS
- 1 pound dried pinto beans
- 6 cups water
- 1 ham hock, or a meaty leftover ham bone
- 1 medium onion, chopped
- 3 cloves garlic, minced
- 1 1/2 teaspoons salt
- 1 pound andouille smoked sausage, or similar smoked sausage, sliced
- 1 (14 1/2-ounce) can of tomatoes, diced
- 1 (4-ounce) can of mild green chile peppers, or a mixture of mild and jalapeño, diced
- 1/2 teaspoon red pepper flakes, crushed, optional
- 4 cups cooked white rice, long-grain, or quick grits, hot boiled

DIRECTIONS
a) The night before put the pinto beans in a large bowl or pot and cover with water to a depth of about 3 inches above the beans. Let them stand for 8 hours or overnight. Drain well.
b) Combine the soaked and drained beans with water, ham hock, onion, and garlic in a large saucepan or Dutch oven over high heat; bring to a boil. Cover and reduce the heat to medium; cook the beans for 45 minutes, or until the beans are tender.*
c) Add the salt, sliced sausage, tomatoes, mild chile peppers, and crushed red pepper flakes, if desired. Cover, reduce heat to low, and simmer for 1 hour, stirring occasionally.
d) Remove the ham hock and remove the meat from the bone. Shred the ham with a fork or chop. Return the ham to the bean mixture.
e) Serve the pinto beans over hot cooked rice.

30. Gallopinto (Nicaraguan Rice and Beans)

Servings:: 8 servings

INGREDIENTS
For the beans
- 1 (16-ounce) bag dried Pinto beans
- Salt
- 7 garlic cloves, peeled

For the rice
- 1/4 cup vegetable oil, divided
- 1 medium yellow onion, finely chopped (about 1 cup), divided
- 1 1/2 cups long-grain white rice
- 3 cups water or low-sodium chicken broth
- 1/2 green bell pepper, cored and seeded

DIRECTIONS
For the beans:
a) Spread beans out on a rimmed baking sheet. Pick out any debris and broken beans. Transfer beans to a colander and rinse under cold running water. Place rinsed beans in a large pot and cover with cold water; let soak for 30 minutes.
b) Bring to boil over high heat. Reduce heat to medium and simmer beans for 30 minutes. Turn off heat, cover beans, and let rest for 1 hour. Bring beans back up to boil over high heat. Add 2 teaspoons salt and garlic, reduce heat to medium, and simmer until beans are tender 30 to 60 minutes.

For the rice:
c) Heat 2 tablespoons oil in a large heavy-bottomed saucepan over medium heat until shimmering. Add 2/3 of onion and cook, stirring, until softened and translucent, about 5 minutes.
d) Add rice and cook, stirring, until grains are shiny and evenly coated with oil, 2 to 3 minutes. Add water or broth and 1 1/2 teaspoons salt, increase heat to high, and bring to a boil. Place bell pepper on top of rice.
e) Boil rice without stirring until most of the liquid has evaporated and you can see small bubbles bursting on the surface of the

rice. Immediately reduce the heat to the lowest setting, cover, and cook (do not stir, do not remove lid) for 15 minutes. Remove and discard bell pepper. Fluff rice with chopsticks or fork, then let cool and refrigerate for 1 day.

For the gallopinto:

f) Heat the remaining 2 tablespoons of oil in a large saucepan over medium-high heat until shimmering. Add remaining onion and cook, stirring, until softened and translucent, about 5 minutes.

g) Add rice and 2 cups beans to skillet and cook, stirring, until rice is evenly coated. Continue to cook, stirring, to allow flavors to meld and the mixture to become slightly crisp, about 10 minutes. Cover and cook over low heat for an additional 10 minutes.

31. Bean sauce & tomatoes over rice

Servings: 6 servings

INGREDIENTS
- 1 cup pinto beans, soaked
- 2 Serrano chilies, seeded & chopped
- ½ tablespoon Ginger, grated
- 1 each Bay leaf
- ¼ teaspoon Turmeric
- 4 cups Water
- 1⅓ cup Stock
- ¼ cup Cilantro
- Salt & pepper
- 2 tablespoons Pecans, chopped & toasted
- 2 tablespoons Olive oil
- 4 Tomatoes, diced
- 1 teaspoon Chili powder
- 1 tablespoon fresh marjoram
- 1 teaspoon Maple syrup
- 5 cups Water
- 1½ cup Long-grain Rice
- 2 Carrots, shredded
- 1 each 3" cinnamon stick
- ½ tablespoon Olive oil

DIRECTIONS
a) Cook beans for 1½ to 2 hours, until the beans are tender. Discard bay leaf &
SAUCE:
b) Combine drained beans, chilies, ginger, bay leaf, turmeric & water in a large pot.
c) Bring to a boil, reduce heat, cover & cook.
d) Place beans, stock & cilantro in a food processor & pulse into a chunky sauce. Season, add pecans & reheat slightly.
TOMATOES:

e) Combine tomatoes, chili powder, marjoram & syrup in a sauté pan. Season with salt & pepper & stir-fry over moderate heat till the tomato begins to caramelize, about 10 minutes. Keep warm on low heat.
   RICE:
f) Boil water, and stir in rice, carrots & cinnamon. Cook until the rice is tender, 10 to 12 minutes if using white rice. Drain & discard cinnamon & rinse briefly under running water.
g) Return to pan & toss with oil.
h) To serve, spoon rice onto warm plates, top with bean sauce & scatter with tomatoes.

32. Cajun pinto beans

Servings: 8

INGREDIENTS
- 1 each Small bag of pinto beans, washed and picked through
- ¼ cup Flour
- ¼ cup Bacon grease
- 1 large Onion, chopped
- 6 cloves Garlic, chopped
- ½ cup Celery, chopped
- 1 each Bay leaf
- ¼ cup Chili powder
- 2 tablespoons ground cumin
- 1 can of tomatoes with chiles
- Salt to taste
- 2 pounds Ham hock or salt pork OPTIONAL
- Chopped cilantro
- 2 cups Long-grain rice, cooked

DIRECTIONS

a) Pick through pinto beans and wash. Soak 1 small bag of pinto beans overnight in cold water and 1 tablespoon of baking soda. Rinse beans and cook for 1 hour. Change the water and add 1 tablespoon of baking soda again. Cook for another hour or two and change the water for the last time, add baking soda, and cook till done.
b) Fry ¼ cup flour and ¼ cup bacon grease into the dark roux (color of cocoa). Add and stir the following until wilted: 1 large chopped onion, 5 or 6 cloves chopped garlic, ½ cup chopped celery, 1 bay leaf, and cilantro.
c) Add chili powder, cumin, and tomatoes with chilies and salt to taste.
d) May be cooked with ham hock or salt pork.
e) Using this roux adds a truly great flavor to pinto beans.
f) Serve with long-grain rice.

33. Rice & beans with cheese

Servings: 5

INGREDIENTS
- 1⅓ cup Water
- 1 cup Shredded Carrots
- 1 teaspoon instant chicken bouillon
- ¼ teaspoon Salt
- 15 ounces Can Pinto   Beans, drained
- 8 ounces Plain lo-fat Yogurt
- ½ cup Shredded low-fat Cheddar cheese
- ⅔ cup Long-grain Rice
- ½ cup Sliced Green Onions
- ½ teaspoon Ground Coriander
- 1 teaspoon Hot pepper Sauce
- 1 cup Low-fat Cottage Cheese
- 1 tablespoon Snipped fresh parsley

DIRECTIONS

a) In a large saucepan combine water, rice, carrots, green onions, bouillon granules, coriander, salt, and bottled hot pepper sauce.
b) Bring to boiling; reduce heat. Cover and simmer for 15 minutes or till rice is tender and water is absorbed.
c) Stir in pinto or navy beans, cottage cheese, yogurt, and parsley.
d) Spoon into a 10x6x2" baking dish.
e) Bake, covered, in a 350 deg F. oven for 20-25 minutes or till heated through. Sprinkle with cheddar cheese. Bake, uncovered, for 3-5 minutes more or till cheese melts.

34. Pinto Beans and Saffron Rice

Servings: 4

INGREDIENTS
Beans
- 3 cups dried pinto beans
- 1/2 stick butter
- 1/3 cup lard
- 1/2 cup sofrito
- 1 large onion diced
- 3 quarts water

Rice
- 1-1/2 cup long-grain rice
- 3 cups chicken broth
- 1/2 teaspoon saffron threads
- 1-1/2 teaspoon kosher salt
- 1/2 cup water
- 1 tablespoon butter
- Vinegar Hot pepper sauce

DIRECTIONS
a) Wash the beans and remove all foreign objects such as stones and bad beans.
b) Dice the onions.
c) Add the onion, beans, sofrito, water, and butter.
d) Let it heat for 4 minutes and add the lard.
e) Cover and boil for 15 minutes stir, cover again, and reduce heat by half. Cook till beans are tender and then add salt.
f) Melt the butter and add the rice. Stir well and add the saffron, broth, and water.
g) Boil the rice stirring occasionally then when the liquids are absorbed cover and remove from heat don't disturb for 20 minutes.
h) Serve with the beans over the rice. Add the vinegar and hot pepper sauce.

35. Taco Seasoning rice with pinto beans

Servings: 6 Servings

INGREDIENTS
- 2 cups Water
- 8 ounces of Tomato sauce
- 1 pack taco seasoning mix
- 1 cup Corn
- ½ cup Green pepper -- chopped
- ½ teaspoon Oregano
- ⅛ teaspoon Garlic powder
- 1 cup long-grain rice
- 16 ounces Pinto beans, canned

DIRECTIONS

a) In a medium saucepan, combine all ingredients, except rice & beans.
b) Bring mixture to a boil over medium heat. Stir in rice and beans.
c) When mixture boils again, stir, then reduce heat to medium-low, cover, and simmer until most of the liquid has cooked out, 45 minutes to 1 hour.
d) Remove from heat, and set aside covered for 5 minutes.
e) Mix well.

36. Indian pumpkin rice and beans

Servings: 8

INGREDIENTS
- 1 tablespoon Canola oil
- 1 medium Yellow onion; chopped
- 2 Clove garlic; minced
- 2 cups Pumpkin cubes
- 2 teaspoons Curry powder
- ½ teaspoon Black pepper
- ½ teaspoon Salt
- ¼ teaspoon Ground cloves
- 1½ cup long-grain white rice
- 1 cup Coarsely chopped kale or spinach
- 15 ounces Cooked pinto beans; drained and rinsed

DIRECTIONS
a) In a large saucepan heat the oil over medium heat.
b) Add the onion and garlic and cook, stirring, for 5 minutes until the onion is translucent. Stir in the pumpkin, curry, pepper, salt, and clove, and cook for 1 minute more.
c) Add 3 cups of water and the rice, cover, and bring to a simmer. Cook over medium-low heat for about 15 minutes.
d) Stir in the kale and beans and cook for about 5 minutes more.
e) Fluff the rice and turn off the heat. Let stand for 10 to 15 minutes before serving.

37. Mexican Cowboy Beans

Servings: 6

INGREDIENTS
- ½ lb. Pinto beans, dried
- 1 Onion, white, large
- 3 cloves Garlic, crushed
- 2 sprigs Cilantro
- ¼ cup Vegetable stock or water
- 6 oz. (3/4 cup) Vegan chorizo
- 2 Serrano chiles, minced
- 1 Tomato, large, diced

DIRECTIONS

h) Soak beans in water overnight.

i) The next day, strain them and place them in a large pot. Pour enough water into the pot to fill ¾ of the way.

j) Cut your onion in half. Place ½ the onion, cilantro sprigs, and 3 garlic cloves into the pot with the beans. Reserve the other half of the onion.

k) Bring water to a simmer and let beans cook until almost tender, approximately 1 ½ hours.

l) While the beans are cooking heat a large sauté pan to medium-high heat. Add chorizo and sauté until slightly browned, about 4 minutes. While the chorizo is cooking, dice the other half of the onion.

m) Remove chorizo from pan and set aside. Add ¼ cup of water, diced onion, and Serrano peppers to the sauté pan. Sweat onion and chiles until tender and translucent about 4 – 5 minutes. Add tomato and let cook for 7-8 minutes more or until the tomato has broken down and released all of its juices.

n) Add this mixture and the chorizo to the pot of beans and let simmer for 20 more minutes or until beans are completely tender. Season to taste with salt and pepper.

o) Before serving, remove the half onion, cilantro sprig, and garlic cloves from the beans. Season with salt and pepper

38. Caribbean Feast

INGREDIENTS
JERK JACKFRUIT
- 3 tins Young Jack Fruit in brine, drained & patted dry then pulled into bit sized pieces
- 1 tablespoons Vita Coca Coconut Oil
- 3 Spring Onions, finely sliced
- 3 Cloves Garlic, minced
- 1/2 Scotch Bonnet Chili (use a full 1 for extra spicy)
- Thumb sized piece ginger, minced
- 1 Yellow Pepper, deseeded & cubed
- 1 cup/200g Black Beans, from a tin. Drained & rinsed.
- 1 tablespoons All Spice
- 2 teaspoon Ground Cinnamon
- 3 tablespoons Soy Sauce
- 5 tablespoons Tomato Purée
- 4 tablespoons Coconut Sugar
- 1 cup/240ml Pineapple Juice
- Juice 1 lime
- 1 tablespoons Fresh Thyme Leaves
- 2 teaspoon Sea Salt
- 1 teaspoon Cracked Black Pepper

RICE & PEAS
- 1 Tin Kidney Beans, liquid reserved
- 1 Tin Coconut Milk
- 3 tablespoons Fresh Thyme
- Pinch Sea Salt & Black Pepper
- 1 & 1/2 cups/340g Long Grain Rice, rinsed
- Vegetable stock, if needed.

FRIED PLANTAIN
- 2 Plantain, peeled & cut into cm discs
- 2 tablespoons Vita Coca Coconut Oil
- 2 tablespoons Coconut Sugar
- Pinch Salt & Pepper

MANGO SALAD
- 1/2 Fresh Mango, peeled and cubed

- 1 teaspoon Fresh Chili, chopped fine
- Handful Fresh Coriander
- Juice of Half a Lime
- Fresh Mixed Salad

DIRECTIONS

a) First up place a large casserole dish or frying pan over a medium heat. Add the coconut oil followed by the onion, garlic, ginger, chili & yellow pepper. Allow the mix to soften for 3 minutes before adding the spices & cooking for 2 more minutes. Add a pinch of seasoning.

b) Add the jackfruit to the pan and stir well, cook the mix for 3-4 minutes.

c) Next add the coconut sugar & the black beans. Keep stirring then add the soy sauce, tomato purée & pineapple juice. Turn the heat down low & add the lime juice plus some chopped fresh thyme leaves.

d) Pop the lid on and allow the jackfruit to cook for around 12-15 minutes.

e) For the rice, add the ingredients to a saucepan and pop the lid on. place the pan over a low heat and allow the rice to absorb all the liquid until it's light & fluffy. this should take 10-12 minutes. if your rice gets too dry before it has cooked, add some water or vegetable stock.

f) next up, the plantain. pre heat a non-stick frying pan over a medium heat & add the coconut oil, when hot add the plantain wedges, and cook on both sides for 3-4 minutes until caramelized & golden. season with coconut sugar, salt & pepper.

g) for the salad simple mix all the ingredients together in a small mixing bowl.

h) serve everything together, enjoy.

39. Jamaican Jerk Jackfruit & Beans with Rice

Servings: 2

INGREDIENTS
- 1 onion
- 2 garlic cloves
- 1 chilli
- 2 vine tomatoes
- 2 teaspoon Jamaican jerk seasoning
- 400g tin of kidney beans
- 400g tin of jackfruit
- 200ml coconut milk
- 150g white long-grain rice
- 50g baby leaf spinach
- Sea salt
- Freshly ground pepper
- 1 tablespoons olive oil
- 300ml boiling water

DIRECTIONS

a) Peel and finely chop the onion. Peel and grate the garlic cloves. Halve the chilli, flicking out the seeds and membrane for less heat, and finely chop. Roughly chop the tomatoes.

b) Pour1 tablespoons oil into a large pan and bring to a medium heat. Slide in the onions and a good pinch of salt and pepper. Fry for 4-5 minutes, stirring occasionally, till softened and slightly coloured. Stir in the garlic, chilli and 2 teaspoon Jamaican jerk seasoning and continue to fry for a further 2 minutes

c) Tip the chopped tomatoes into the pan. Drain the kidney beans and jackfruit and add them to the pan. Pour in the coconut milk. Combine well and bring to the boil, then partly cover with a lid and simmer gently for 20 minutes During the cooking time, use a wooden spoon every now and then to break up the jackfruit chunks a little.

d) Tip the rice into a sieve and give it a good rinse under cold water. Tip into a small pan and add 300ml boiling water and a pinch of salt. Pop on a lid and bring to the boil, then turn right down and very gently simmer for 8 minutes, till all the water has been absorbed. Take the rice off the heat and leave it to steam in the pan, covered, for 10 minutes

e) Stir the spinach into the jackfruit and beans till wilted. Have a taste of the sauce and add more salt if needed.

f) Spoon the rice into a couple of deep bowls and top with generous ladlefuls of the jackfruit curry and serve.

40. Rice Pilaf With Bean, Fruits And Nuts

INGREDIENTS

- 1 1/2 cups long-grain rice
- 1 tablespoon neutral vegetable oil
- 1 medium onion, finely chopped
- 1 to 2 small fresh hot chili peppers, sliced, optional
- 2/3 cup raisins or dried cranberries, or a combination
- 1/3 cup cooked pinto beans
- 1/3 cup finely chopped dried apricots
- 1/4 teaspoon turmeric
- 1/2 teaspoon cinnamon
- 1/4 teaspoon ground or fresh nutmeg
- 1/2 teaspoon dried basil
- 1/4 cup orange juice, preferably fresh
- 2 teaspoons agave nectar
- 1 to 2 tablespoons lemon or lime juice, to taste
- 1/2 cup toasted cashews (whole or chopped) or sliced almonds
- Salt and freshly ground pepper to taste

DIRECTIONS

a) Combine the rice with 4 cups water in a saucepan. Bring to a gentle boil, then lower the heat, cover, and simmer gently for 30 minutes, or until the water is absorbed.

b) Once the rice is done, heat the oil in a large skillet. Add the onion and optional chili peppers sauté over medium heat until golden.

c) Stir in the rice and all the remaining ingredients except the nuts, salt, and pepper. cook over low heat, stirring frequently, for about 8 to 10 minutes, allowing the flavors to blend.

d) Stir in the nuts, season with salt and pepper, and serve.

41. Beans and rice cha cha cha bowl

Servings: 6

INGREDIENTS
- 2 tablespoons Olive oil
- 2 Cloves garlic, minced
- 1 cup Sliced onion
- 1 cup Peeled, sliced celery
- 1 cup Sliced carrots
- 1 teaspoon Chili powder
- ¼ cup Canned diced green chiles
- 1 pounds pinto beans
- ¼ Onion, roughly sliced
- 1 Fat 263 Calories
- 2 cups Sliced mushrooms
- 2 cups Cooked basic black beans
- ½ cup Reserve bean stock
- 2 tablespoons Chopped cilantro
- Salt and pepper to taste
- 3 cups Cooked long-grain rice
- 1 tablespoon Lemon juice
- 2 teaspoons Salt or to taste

INGREDIENTS
a) In large deep saucepan heat olive oil, and sauté garlic, onion, celery, carrots and chili powder, until onion is translucent.
b) Add chiles and mushrooms and sauté 5 minutes more.
c) Stir in beans, bean stock and cilantro. Season to taste.
d) Cover and simmer over low heat about 10 minutes, stirring occasionally.
e) Serve over rice.

42. Turnip Stir Fry with Beans

Servings: 2 people

INGREDIENTS
- 1 tablespoon olive oil
- 2 purple top turnips - scrubbed, trimmed, and diced
- 3 cups spinach
- 1 15.5 oz can pinto beans - drained and rinsed
- 1 tablespoon fresh ginger - finely chopped
- 2 cloves garlic - pressed or minced
- 1 tablespoon honey
- 1 tablespoon rice vinegar
- 2 tablespoon reduced sodium soy sauce
- 1 cup long-grain rice - cooked, for serving

DIRECTIONS

a) If you need to prepare rice or a whole grain for the meal, start that before making the stir fry.
b) Heat olive oil in a large skillet over medium heat. Add the turnips and cook, stirring/flipping occasionally, for 8-12 minutes or until lightly browned and tender.
c) While the turnips are cooking, whisk together the ginger, garlic, honey, rice vinegar, and soy sauce in a small bowl. Add the spinach, beans, and sauce to the skillet. Cook for 4-6 minutes, or until the spinach is wilted and the stir fry is heated through.
d) Serve warm over rice.

43. Rice with lamb, dill and beans

Servings: 8 servings

INGREDIENTS
- 2 tablespoons Butter
- 1 medium Onion; peeled and cut into 1/4 inch thick slices
- 3 pounds Boneless lamb shoulder, cubed
- 3 cups Water
- 1 tablespoon Salt
- 2 cups uncooked long grain white rice, soaked and drained
- 4 cups Dill, fresh; finely cut
- 2 ten oz. Pinto beans
- 8 tablespoons Butter; melted
- ¼ teaspoon Saffron threads; pulverized and dissolved in 1 tablespoon. warm water

DIRECTIONS
a) In a heavy 3 to 4 quart casserole, with a tightly fitting lid, melt the 2 tablespoons of butter over moderate heat.
b) When the foam begins to subside, add the onions and, stirring frequently, cook for about 10 minutes, or until the slices are richly browned. With a slotted spoon, transfer them to a plate.
c) A half dozen pieces or so at a time, brown the lamb cubes in the fat remaining in the casserole, turning them with tongs or a spoon and regulating the heat so that they color deeply and evenly without burning. As they brown, transfer the cubes of lamb to the plate with the onions.
d) Pour the 3 cups of water into the casserole and bring to a boil over high heat, meanwhile scraping in the brown particles clinging to the bottom and sides of the pan. Return the lamb and onion to the casserole, add the salt, and reduce the heat to low.
e) Cover tightly and simmer for about 1 hour and 15 minutes, or until the lamb is tender and shows no resistance when pierced with the point of a small, sharp knife. Transfer the lamb, onions

and all the cooking liquid to a large bowl and set the casserole aside.

f) Preheat the oven to 350 degrees. Bring 6 cups of water to a boil in a 5 to 6 quart saucepan. Pour in the rice in a slow, thin stream so the water does not stop boiling. Stir once or twice, boil briskly for 5 minutes, then remove the pan from the heat, stir in the dill and beans and drain in a fine sieve.

g) Ladle about half of the rice mixture into the casserole and moisten it with « cup of the lamb cooking liquid. Then with a spatula or spoon spread the rice mixture to the edges of the pan.

h) With a slotted spoon return the lamb and onions to the casserole and smooth them over the rice.

i) Then spread the remaining rice mixture on top. Combine 2 tablespoons of the melted butter with 6 tablespoons of the lamb broth and pour it over the rice. Bring the casserole to a boil over high heat.

j) Cover tightly and bake in the middle of the oven for 30 to 40 minutes, or until the beans are tender and the rice has absorbed all the liquid in the casserole.

k) To serve, spoon about a cup of the rice mixture into a small bowl, add the dissolved saffron and stir until the rice is bright yellow.

l) Spread about half the remaining rice on a heated platter and arrange the lamb over it. Cover the lamb with the rest of the plain rice mixture and garnish it with the saffron rice. Pour the remaining 6 tablespoons of melted butter over the top.

44. Cheesy Pinto Beans

Servings: 4

INGREDIENTS
- 2 cloves garlic
- 1 jalapeño
- 1 tablespoon cooking oil
- 2 15oz. cans pinto beans
- 1/4 teaspoon smoked paprika
- 1/4 teaspoon ground cumin
- 1/8 teaspoon freshly cracked black pepper
- 2 dashes hot sauce
- 1/2 cup shredded cheddar cheese
- 2 servings long-grain rice, cooked

DIRECTIONS
a) Mince the garlic and finely dice the jalapeño.
b) Add the garlic, jalapeño, and cooking oil to a pot. Sauté the garlic and jalapeño over medium heat for about one minute, or just until the garlic is very fragrant.
c) Add one can of pinto beans to a blender, with the liquid in the can, and purée until smooth.
d) Add the puréed beans and the second can of beans (drained) to the sauce-pot with the garlic and jalapeño. Stir to combine.
e) Season the beans with the smoked paprika, cumin, pepper, and hot sauce. Stir to combine, then heat through over medium, stirring occasionally.
f) Finally, add the shredded cheddar and stir until it has melted smoothly into the beans. Taste the beans and adjust the seasoning to your liking. Serve over rice or with your favorite meal.

45. Rice and beans with basil pesto

Servings: 4 Servings

INGREDIENTS
- Vegetable cooking spray
- 1 cup Chopped onion
- 1 cup Uncooked long-grain rice
- 13¾ ounce No-salt-added chicken broth, (1 can)
- 1 cup Chopped unpeeled tomato
- ¼ cup Commercial pesto basil sauce
- 16 ounces pinto beans

DIRECTIONS
a) Coat a large skillet with cooking spray, and place over medium-high heat until hot.
b) Add onion; sauté 2 minutes. Add rice and broth; bring to a boil.
c) Reduce heat, and simmer, uncovered, 15 minutes or until rice is done and liquid is absorbed.
d) Stir in tomato, pesto sauce, and beans; cook 2 minutes or until thoroughly heated.

46. Flank steak with black beans and rice

Servings: 6 Servings
INGREDIENTS
- 1½ pounds Flank steak
- 3 tablespoons Vegetable oil
- 2 Bay leaves
- 5 cups Beef stock
- 4 tablespoons Olive oil
- 2 Onions; chopped
- 6 Garlic cloves; minced
- 1 tablespoon Dried oregano
- 1 tablespoon Ground cumin
- 2 Tomatoes; seeded, chopped
- Salt; to taste
- Freshly-ground black pepper; to taste
- Pinto beans
- Cooked white rice
- 2 tablespoons Vegetable oil
- 6 Eggs

DIRECTIONS

a) Season steak with salt and pepper. Heat vegetable oil in heavy large skillet over high heat. Add steak and cook until browned on all sides. Add bay leaves and stock.
b) Reduce heat and simmer slowly until steak is very tender, turning occasionally, about 2 hours.
c) Remove from heat and allow meat to cool in stock. Remove meat from stock and shred it. Reserve 1 cup cooking liquid; reserve remaining cooking liquid for another use. Heat olive oil in heavy large skillet over medium-high heat. Add onion and sauté until golden.
d) Add garlic, oregano and cumin and sauté until fragrant. Add tomatoes and continue to cook until most of liquid evaporates.
e) Add shredded meat and 1 cup reserved cooking liquid. Season to taste with salt and pepper. Arrange the beef, rice and beans on a rectangular platter in three rows with the rice in the center (it should look like the Venezuelan flag).
f) Heat vegetable oil in heavy large skillet over medium heat. Crack eggs into skillet. Fry until softly set. Serve atop beans, meat and rice.

47. African Rice and Beans

Servings: 6

INGREDIENTS
- ½ cup red / palm / or canola oil I used ½ and ½
- 2-3 garlic clove minced
- 1 medium onion diced
- 1 tablespoon smoked paprika
- 1 teaspoon dried thyme
- ½ scotch bonnet pepper or ½ teaspoon cayenne pepper
- 4 tomatoes diced
- 2 cups washed long grain rice
- 2 cups cooked beans black, red, black-eyed peas
- 4 1/2 - 5 cups chicken broth or water
- 1 tablespoon salt or more to taste
- 1/4 cup crayfish optional
- 1 teaspoon chicken bouillon optional

DIRECTIONS

a) Heat a saucepan with oil. Then add onions, garlic, thyme, smoked paprika and hot pepper, sauté for about a minute, add tomatoes. Cook for about 5-7 minutes.
b) Stir in rice to the pan; continue stirring for about 2 minutes.
c) Then add beans , 4 1/2 cups of chicken stock/water, bring to a boil reduce heat, and simmer until rice is cooked, about 18 minutes or more. Adjust for salt and pepper. You have to stir occasionally to be preventing any burns.
d) Serve warm with chicken, stew or vegetables

48. Tumbleweed, pinto bean, and rice salad

Servings: 6 servings

INGREDIENTS
- ¾ cup Dried pinto beans
- 1½ cup Tumbleweed greens or curly endive, or fennel tops, washed thoroughly and drained
- 1½ cup Cooked white long-grain rice
- ¾ cup Sunflower oil
- 3 tablespoons Herb flavored red wine vinegar
- 2 tablespoons chopped fresh chives
- 2 smalls Garlic cloves, peeled
- ¼ teaspoon Black pepper
- ⅛ teaspoon Salt
- Chive blossoms for garnish

DIRECTIONS
a) Soak the beans overnight in water to cover. In the morning, drain the beans, rinse them under cold running water, and place them in a saucepan with fresh water to cover.
b) Bring to a boil over high heat, then reduce the heat and simmer for several hours until the beans are soft and the skins begin to split.
c) Add water when necessary to keep the beans from drying, and stir occasionally to prevent them from burning and sticking. Remove from the heat, drain, and allow to cool.
d) In a bowl, toss together the greens, beans, and rice. Cover and chill in the refrigerator for at least 30 minutes.
e) In a blender, combine the oil, vinegar, chives, garlic, pepper, and salt. Blend at high speed until the chives and garlic are finely puréed.
f) Pour the dressing over the salad, toss, and garnish with chive blossoms.

49. Pinto Bean, Rice, and Veggie Salad

Servings: 4

INGREDIENTS
- 2 cups water
- 1 cup uncooked long-grain rice
- 15-ounce can of pinto beans, rinsed and drained
- 1 red bell pepper
- 1 yellow bell pepper
- 5 green onions
- ¼ cup olive oil
- ¼ cup apple cider vinegar
- 1 tablespoon Dijon mustard
- 1 teaspoon ground cumin
- 1 large garlic clove
- ¾ teaspoon kosher salt
- ¼ teaspoon freshly ground black pepper

DIRECTIONS

a) Pour 2 cups of water into a medium saucepan. Bring to a boil, then add the uncooked rice, stir to combine, and return to a boil. Cover the pan, and reduce heat as low as possible.

b) Simmer without opening the lid for 15 minutes, until the rice is tender and the water is absorbed.

c) Finely chop the peppers. Thinly slice the green onions. Mince the garlic.

d) In a large mixing bowl, combine the cooked rice, beans, chopped red and yellow peppers, and scallions, and toss to combine.

e) In a small bowl or measuring cup, combine the olive oil, apple cider vinegar, mustard, cumin, garlic, salt, and black pepper, Whisk thoroughly to combine, then pour over the rice mixture.

f) Toss gently to coat, then either serve immediately or keep refrigerated for up to 3 days.

50. Edamame And Pinto Bean Salad

SERVINGS: 6

INGREDIENTS
FOR THE DRESSING
- 1/2 cup cider vinegar
- 1/4 cup olive oil
- 1 1/2 teaspoons cumin
- 1 teaspoon fresh minced garlic
- Salt and pepper to taste

FOR THE SALAD
- 3 cups cooked long-grain rice, cooled
- 2 cups edamame beans
- 1 oz can pinto beans rinsed
- 3/4 cup finely diced red pepper
- 3/4 cup fresh cilantro roughly chopped
- Salt and pepper to taste

DIRECTIONS

a) In a bowl with a whisk, combine the olive oil, vinegar, garlic, and cumin. Whisk until well combined, taste, and season with salt and pepper. Set aside.
b) In a separate large bowl, add the cooled rice, edamame beans, chopped pepper, and pinto beans.
c) Mix and season with salt and pepper. Add the chopped cilantro.
d) Do not add the dressing just before serving. Add about half at first and taste. Add more if you prefer.
e) Mix well and serve in a large bowl, garnished with more cilantro leaves.

51. Rice & bean salad with minced crudite

Servings: 4

INGREDIENTS
- 1¼ cup Cooked Long-grain rice
- 1 cup Cooked pinto beans -- rinsed And drained
- 2 tablespoons Chopped pecans -- roasted
- 2 tablespoons minced red bell pepper
- 2 tablespoons minced red onion
- 3 tablespoons minced fresh cilantro
- 3 tablespoons Green chili peppers, diced
- ⅓ cup Carrots -- minced
- ⅓ cup Broccoli florets -- minced
- ⅓ cup Cauliflower florets, Minced
- Salt and pepper -- freshly Ground
- 2 cups Iceberg lettuce -- shredded
- 3 tablespoons Fat-free Italian salad

DIRECTIONS

a) Cook pinto beans, with a garnish of celery stalk, carrot chunk, and fennel stalk. Rinse, drain, chill.
b) About two to three hours before serving, combine the chilled rice and beans in a large mixing bowl. Peel a carrot and cut it into 1-inch pieces.
c) Finely chop, along with 5 to 6 broccoli florets and cauliflower florets, in a food processor. Add to the bowl and toss.
d) Dry-pan roast the pecans pieces for about 4 minutes over medium heat. Remove from heat. Let cool and then add to salad.
e) Mince by hand the onion, the red bell pepper, and the fresh cilantro leaves. Chop the canned chili peppers.
f) Add to salad and toss well. Taste and season with salt and pepper. Toss well.
g) Add 3 tablespoons of salad dressing. Toss. Chill. Serve on a bed of thinly shredded lettuce.

52. Bean and Rice Soup

Servings: 4

INGREDIENTS
- 2 cups chicken, cooked and cubed
- 1 cup long-grain rice, cooked
- 2 15-ounce cans of pinto beans, drained
- 4 cup chicken stock
- 2 tablespoon Taco Seasoning Mix
- 1 cup tomato sauce

Toppings:
- Grated cheese
- Salsa
- Chopped cilantro
- Chopped onion

DIRECTIONS

a) Place all ingredients in a medium stockpot. Stir gently.
b) Cook over medium heat, simmering for about 20 minutes, stirring occasionally.
c) Serve with toppings.

53. Chili con Carne

INGREDIENTS
- Ground/minced beef 500g
- 1 Large onion chopped
- 3 Cloves of Garlic
- 2 Tins of chopped tomatoes 400g
- Squeeze of tomato purée
- 1 teaspoon of chili powder (or to taste)
- 1 teaspoon of ground cumin
- dash of Worcester sauce
- Sprinkle of salt and pepper
- 1 Chopped red pepper
- 1 tin of drained kidney beans 400g

DIRECTIONS

a) Fry the onion in a hot pan with oil until nearly brown then add chopped garlic

b) Add the mince and stir until brown; drain any excess fat if desired

c) Add all dried spices and seasoning then reduce heat and add chopped tomatoes

d) Stir well and add tomato purée and Worcestershire sauce then leave to simmer for about an hour (less if you're in a rush)

e) Add the chopped red pepper and continue to simmer for 5 minutes, then add the tin of drained kidney beans and cook for a further 5 minutes If the chili become to dry at any point just add a bit of water.

f) Serve with rice, jacket potatoes or pasta!

54. Vegan Rice Soup

Servings: 4

INGREDIENTS
- 4 large celery stalks
- 3 large carrots
- 1 medium white onion
- 1 teaspoon dried thyme
- 1 teaspoon dried parsley
- 1 teaspoon garlic powder
- 1 teaspoon salt
- 1/2 teaspoon ground sage
- 1 tablespoon coconut aminos
- 4 cups vegetable broth
- 2 cups water
- 2/3 cup long-grain white rice
- 1 can pinto beans (15 oz. can)

DIRECTIONS
a) Dice or chop the veggies into bite size pieces.
b) Add large pot to stove and turn on medium heat. Spray the bottom of the pot with avocado oil or olive oil spray. Add veggies.
c) Cook the veggies 3-4 minutes.
d) After 3-4 minutes, add spices, bay leaf and coconut aminos. Stir and cook 1-2 more minutes.
e) While veggies are cooking, rinse the rice well.
f) Add 1/2 cup of vegetable broth and scrape the bottom/side of the pot removing any brown bits from the bottom.
g) Add the rest of the broth, water and rice to the pot. Stir and cover. Turn the heat up to high.
h) Once the soup comes up to a boil, turn down the heat to low and cook for 15 minutes.
i) While the soup is cooking, rinse and drain the beans. And add them to the soup.
j) Right before serving, remove the bay leaves. Serve hot.

55. Bean and rice burritos

Servings: 10 servings

INGREDIENTS
- 1 can of Pinto beans
- 1 cup long-grain rice; cooked
- ½ cup Onions; frozen, chopped
- ½ cup peppers; frozen, chopped
- ½ cup Corn; frozen
- Chili powder; dash
- Lettuce, chopped
- 1 bunch of Scallions; chopped
- Cumin; dash
- Garlic powder; dash
- ¾ cup Water
- Salsa, oil-free, low sodium
- 10 Tortillas, whole wheat
- 1 Tomato; chopped

DIRECTIONS

a) Sauté the frozen onions and green peppers in a few tablespoons of water in a skillet.

b) Drain and rinse the beans and place them in a skillet and mash with a potato masher. Add the cooked rice, corn, spices, and water. Heat 5 to 10 minutes until most of the water is absorbed, stirring occasionally.

c) Heat the tortillas quickly (just to soften) in a preheated skillet, a toaster oven, or a microwave.

d) Place a line of bean mixture down the middle of each tortilla, and add a teaspoon of salsa and any of the other toppings as desired.

e) Fold up ½ inch on each side, tuck in the top edge, and roll into a burrito. Serve immediately, topped with additional salsa if desired.

56. Rice and Bean Roll-Ups

Servings: 6

INGREDIENTS
- 1 1/2 cups salsa
- 1 cup cooked long-grain rice
- 2 medium Roma (plum) tomatoes, chopped
- 1 small bell pepper, cut into 1/2-inch pieces
- 1 can (15 oz) black beans with cumin, undrained
- 1 can (7 ounces) whole kernel corn, drained
- 6 garden vegetable-flavored flour tortillas, (8 inches in diameter)
- 1 cup shredded Mexican cheese blend (4 ounces)

DIRECTIONS

a) Heat oven to 350°F. Spread 1/2 cup of the salsa in ungreased rectangular baking dish, 13x9x2 inches.

b) Mix rice, tomatoes, bell pepper, black beans and corn. Spread about 1 cup rice mixture on each tortilla; roll up tortilla. Place seam sides down on salsa in baking dish. Spoon remaining 1 cup salsa over tortillas. Sprinkle with cheese.

c) Cover and bake 30 to 35 minutes or until heated through and cheese is melted.

d) For more spice, use the new jalapeño- or cilantro-flavored tortillas available in the supermarket.

57. Baked Pinto Bean Flautas with rice flour Tortilla

Servings: 25 flautas

INGREDIENTS
- 1/2 cup red onion
- 1/2 cup white onion
- 2 tablespoons avocado oil
- 1 large bell pepper diced
- 2 cups black beans
- 1.5 cups chickpeas
- 1 can pinto beans, drained and rinsed
- 1/4-1/2 cup salsa verde
- 1 tablespoons chili powder
- 1 tablespoons garlic powder
- 1 tablespoons cumin
- 1/8 teaspoon cayenne pepper or paprika
- 1/8 teaspoon oregano
- salt, to taste
- 2-3 tablespoons fresh chopped cilantro
- 2-4 cups of your favorite Mexican cheeses, shredded
- 25-30 small rice flour tortillas

DIRECTIONS

a) Pre-heat your oven to 385 degrees F.
b) Sauté your onion in a little bit of oil [approx 2 tablespoons] to soften.
c) Next combine bell pepper, beans, and salsa in a large bowl.
d) Add onions to the mix and season with chili powder, garlic powder, cumin, cilantro, salt, cayenne, oregano.
e) Next wrap a small stack of corn tortillas [4-5] in a damp paper towel and microwave on high for 30 seconds. Follow it up with an additional 30 seconds.
f) Once steamed, spray or rub one side of the tortilla with oil and add a thin layer of veggie filling vertically along the center of the opposite [un-oiled] of the tortilla. Top it off with a layer of cheese [as much or as little as you want!] and gently roll the tortilla.

g) tip: your steamed tortillas will naturally start to curl around each other in the stack. This is a total advantage since they naturally want to roll! When you unwrap your tortillas from the paper towel, oil the side facing up and then put the filling on the side that is curling inwards. Viola!
h) Seal each flauta shut with two toothpicks and place on a wire baking/cooling rack. Repeat these steps until you have a rack full of flautas.
i) Place them on a wire rack on on a foil-lined baking sheet. The wire rack elevates the flautas and allows them to get nice and crispy on both sides.
j) Sprinkle the finished product with a dash of, garlic powder and cayenne pepper.
k) Bake on the middle rack, at 385F, for approximately 15-18 minutes. At the very end, set oven to broil on HIGH for just under a minute to crisp the tortillas into a perfectly golden, crunchy shell.

58. Bean and rice burgers

Servings: 4 servings

INGREDIENTS
- 1 cup Cooked long-grain rice
- 1½ cup Cooked pinto beans, mashed
- ½ cup Wheat flour (or white)
- 1 tablespoon Margarine or butter
- 1 medium Onion -- diced
- 1 Clove garlic -- mashed
- 1 tablespoon Spike or seasoning salt
- 1 cup Cooked mashed potatoes
- ½ cup Cornmeal
- ½ cup Bran
- ½ cup Cracked wheat
- 1 small Pepper -- diced
- 1 Grated carrot

DIRECTIONS
a) Heat greased grill or electric fry-pan on medium heat.
b) Add all Ingredients and mix well. Look for a 'hamburger' consistency.
c) Spoon about 2 heaping Tablespoons of mix onto grill or fry-pan for each burger and flatten with greased pancake turner.
d) Turn several times rather than just once on each side like conventional burgers, they have a better texture that way.

59. Rice and bean enchiladas with red sauce

Servings: 12 Servings

INGREDIENTS
- 12 9 inch flour tortillas; fat-free

Filling
- 1 tablespoon Canola oil
- 2 Onions; chopped
- 6 Cloves garlic; minced
- 16 ounces Tomato sauce
- 1 tablespoon Chili powder
- ½ teaspoon Red pepper flakes; crushed
- 2 teaspoons Ground cumin
- 2 teaspoons Salt
- 5 cups Cooked rice
- 3 pounds Cooked beans
- Water; as needed
- ⅔ cup Pitted black olives; chopped
- 8 ounces Sharp cheddar cheese; grated
- ½ bunch Chopped cilantro leaves

DIRECTIONS

a) In a large non-stick sauté pan or sauce pan, heat oil. Add onion and garlic and cook until soft. Add tomato sauce, chili powder, pepper flakes, cumin and salt. Cook slowly, uncovered, 15 minutes to blend flavors.

b) Add half of the tomato mixture to the cooked beans in the bowl. Stir to blend. Add the cooked rice to the remaining half of the tomato mixture.

c) Preheat oven to 350F. Lightly oil a very large) or 2 smaller baking dishes. Place a thin layer of Red Sauce, (about 1-1 ½ cups) on bottom of baking dish.

d) Dividing the filling 12 ways, place seasoned beans (about ½ cup), seasoned rice (about ½ cup), chopped olives, cheese and cilantro on each tortilla.

e) Roll tightly and place, seam down, in a single layer in baking dish.
f) Top with remaining Red Sauce. Cover with parchment or wax paper and top tightly with foil. Bake in preheated oven for 60 minutes. Remove foil and paper, sprinkle with 2 oz. of reserved cheese and bake an additional 15 minutes.
g) Serve with Fresh Green Salsa.

60. Rice And Bean Quesadillas

Servings: 4-6

INGREDIENTS
- 1 teaspoon olive oil-
- 1 cup cooked long-grain rice
- 1 (15 oz) can pinto beans, drained and rinsed
- 1 teaspoon cumin
- 1 teaspoon paprika
- 3/4 teaspoon garlic powder
- 1/2 teaspoon onion powder
- 4–6 tortillas
- Sharp Cheddar Shredded cheese

DIRECTIONS

a) Heat a large pan over medium heat and add olive oil, rice, beans and spices. Cook until heated through, about 3 minutes.

b) Lay your tortilla on a cutting board and and sprinkle one half with a small handful of cheese 1/4 – 1/3 cup and then top with an equal amount of rice and bean mixture.

c) Fold tortilla over and place in a lightly greased pan. Cook quesadilla until cheese is melted and each side of the tortilla is golden brown, flipping once.

d) Let quesadillas cool for a few minutes before slicing.

61. Peruvian Tacu Tacu Cake

SERVINGS: 2-4 servings

INGREDIENTS
FOR THE SALSA CRIOLLA
- 1/2 small red onion, thinly sliced
- 2 tablespoons chopped fresh cilantro leaves
- 2 tablespoons fresh lime juice
- 1/4 teaspoon aji Amarillo paste
- 1/4 teaspoon kosher salt

FOR THE TACU TACU
- 3 tablespoons grapeseed or safflower oil
- 1/2 small red onion, chopped
- 2 garlic cloves, chopped
- 1/2 teaspoon kosher salt, plus more to taste
- 1 teaspoon aji Amarillo paste
- 2 cups cooked or canned pinto beans, drained and rinsed
- 1 cup cold cooked long-grain white rice
- 1 tablespoon chopped fresh flat-leaf parsley leaves
- 1 tablespoon chopped fresh oregano
- 1 lime, cut into wedges

DIRECTIONS
a) Make the salsa: In a medium bowl, combine the onion with enough cold water to cover, and let sit for at least 10 minutes, then drain. Toss with the cilantro, lime juice, aji Amarillo and sal

b) Make the tacu tacu: In a 10-inch nonstick skillet over medium-high heat, heat 1 tablespoon of the oil until shimmering. Stir in the onion and garlic and cook, stirring, until lightly browned, 5 to 6 minutes. Stir in the salt and aji Amarillo, and scrape the mixture into the bowl of a food processor. Wipe out the skillet.

c) Add 1 cup of the beans to the food processor and purée briefly until mostly smooth but still chunky. Scrape the mixture into a large bowl.

d) Add the remaining 1 cup of beans (left whole), the rice, parsley, and oregano to the bowl and stir to thoroughly combine. Taste, and add more salt if needed.
e) Return the skillet to medium heat and pour in another 1 tablespoon of oil. Add the rice-and-bean mixture and use a spatula to spread it around evenly and lightly pack it down.
f) Cook until deeply browned on the bottom, about 7 minutes. Remove from the heat, invert a plate (preferably with no rim) on top of the skillet, and carefully flip both over to land the bean-and-rice cake bottom-side up onto the plate.
g) Return the skillet to medium heat, pour in the remaining 1 tablespoon of oil, and slide the cake back into the skillet.
h) Cook for another 7 minutes, or until deeply browned on the other side, then invert the plate and flip the skillet over again to land the cake onto the plate.
i) Top with the salsa and serve hot with lime wedges.

62. Alkaline Stew Peas with Dumplings

Servings: 4

INGREDIENTS
- 1 cup dried pinto beans, soaked overnight
- 1 onion, large
- 1 carrot, large
- 3 garlic cloves
- 1 stalk scallion
- 1 teaspoon thyme
- ½ teaspoon allspice, ground
- 1 tablespoons all-purpose seasoning
- salt and pepper, to taste
- 1 scotch bonnet pepper, whole
- 1 cup coconut milk
- 1 tablespoons oil, optional

GLUTEN FREE DUMPLINGS
- 1½ tablespoons. white rice flour
- 1½ tablespoons. buckwheat flour
- 1 tablespoons potato starch
- ½ tablespoons tapioca flour
- 1 tablespoons almond flour
- ¼ teaspoon salt
- 2 tablespoons. water

DIRECTIONS

f) Drain soaked beans and place in a pressure cooker. Cover with fresh water, about an inch above the beans. Cover and cook for about 20 to 25 minutes.

g) Meanwhile, chop the onion, garlic, carrot and scallion then place in a bowl.

h) In another bowl, combine all the dry ingredients to make the dumplings. Gradually add water, mixing after each pour, until a firm dough starts to form.

i) Divide the dough into about 8 to 10 smaller pieces. Roll each piece between the palms of your hands in the shape of 3-inch

j) long ropes or about the size of your pinkie finger. Set dumplings aside on a plate.
j) Once the beans are cooked, allow the pressure cooker to release pressure before opening. You can run the pot under cool tap water to help.
k) Remove the lid and add the chopped seasonings and remaining spices.
l) Add the coconut milk, dumplings and simmer on low heat for 10 minutes.
m) Add the dumplings then cook for an additional 5 minutes are until the dumplings are fully cooked. If the stew is too thick, add more water as needed.
n) Remove from heat. Serve with rice and steamed veggies or avocado.

63. Bean and rice pudding with raisins and nuts

Servings: 18 Servings

INGREDIENTS
- 1½ cup Rice; Long Grain
- 3/4 cup Mung Beans; Split
- 1/4 Cup pinto bean
- 1 cup Ghee
- 2 cups Milk
- 2½ cup Boiling Water
- 1½ cup Brown Sugar; Packed
- ¼ cup Seedless Raisins; Dark
- ½ cup Cashews; Dry-Roasted, Unsalted, Chopped

DIRECTIONS

a) Rinse and drain the rice.
b) Heat 2 tablespoons of the ghee in a large saucepan. Add the beans and fry, over medium heat, stirring, for 3 minutes or until very lightly colored.
c) Add 2 cups of the boiling water, stir, and lower heat and cook at a simmer, partially covered, for 15 minutes.
d) Add the rice and the additional ½ cup water, and stir. Cook covered, at a low simmer, until the liquid is absorbed and the rice is almost tender (15-20 minutes).
e) Add the milk, bring the mixture to a boil, and cook, stirring often to prevent sticking but being careful to keep the grains whole, until it is thickened and the rice is cooked (about 15 minutes).
f) Add the sugar, cardamom, and raisins, and continue cooking for 3 more minutes. Stir in the remaining ghee 2 tablespoons at a time, and most of the cashew nuts (save some for garnish).
g) Let the pudding rest, covered, for 15 minutes before you serve it
h) Serve warm, at room temperature, or chilled, either as a dessert or as a snack all by itself.

CRAWFISH ÉTOUFFÉE

64. Shrimp Étouffée

Makes: 4 SERVINGS

INGREDIENTS:
- ½ cup salted butter
- ½ cup all-purpose flour
- 1 tablespoon vegetable oil
- 1 large green bell pepper, diced
- ½ medium onion, diced
- 2 stalks celery, diced
- 3 garlic cloves, minced
- 1 (14-ounce) can diced tomatoes
- 1 tablespoon tomato paste
- 2 cups chicken broth or seafood stock
- 2 sprigs of fresh thyme, plus more for garnish
- 1½ teaspoons Creole seasoning
- 1 teaspoon Worcestershire sauce
- ½ teaspoon ground black pepper
- ½ teaspoon red pepper flakes
- 2 pounds raw jumbo shrimp, peeled and deveined
- 2 cups cooked white rice

INSTRUCTIONS:

a) In a large saucepan over medium heat, melt the butter. Once the butter is melted, add in the flour and whisk until everything is well combined. Cook the roux until it reaches a nice, rich brown color, 10 to 15 minutes, but be sure not to burn it!

b) Add in the bell peppers, onions, celery, and garlic. Cook until the veggies soften, 3 to 5 minutes. Then add the diced tomatoes and tomato paste. Slowly pour in the broth and toss in the fresh thyme. Mix until everything is well combined, then sprinkle in the Creole seasoning, Worcestershire sauce, black pepper, and red pepper flakes. Stir the ingredients , and let cook for 5 minutes over medium-high heat.

c) Slowly start adding in the shrimp, and stir. Reduce the heat to low and cook for 5 more minutes. Remove the thyme sprigs. Garnish with thyme and serve with hot rice.

65. Crawfish Étouffée

MAKES 8–10 SERVINGS

INGREDIENTS:
- 3/4 cup butter or vegetable oil
- 3/4 cup all-purpose flour
- 1 large onion, chopped
- 1 bunch green onions, chopped, white and green parts separated
- 1 green bell pepper, chopped
- 3 celery stalks, chopped.
- 4 large garlic cloves, minced
- 3 tablespoons tomato paste
- 6 cups seafood stock or water
- ½ teaspoon dried thyme
- 3 bay leaves
- 1 teaspoon Creole seasoning
- 1 teaspoon salt
- 1 tablespoon fresh lemon juice
- Cayenne pepper and freshly ground black pepper, to taste
- 2–3 pounds crawfish tails with fat
- 3 tablespoons chopped flat-leaf parsley
- Cooked long-grain white rice, for serving

INSTRUCTIONS:

a) In a large, heavy pot, melt the butter or heat the oil over medium heat. Add the flour and stir constantly. If using butter, cook the roux until it turns a blonde or golden color. If using oil, continue cooking, stirring, until the roux is medium brown. Add the onions, the white parts of the green onions, the bell peppers, the celery, and the garlic and sauté, stirring, until translucent.

b) Add the tomato paste, stock or water, thyme, bay leaves, Creole seasoning, salt, and lemon juice, season with the cayenne and pepper, and bring to a boil. Reduce the heat, cover, and simmer for 20 minutes, stirring occasionally and skimming any fat off the top. Add the crawfish, parsley, and green onion tops, bring to a boil, reduce the heat, and simmer for 10 minutes. Remove the bay leaves.

c) When ready to serve, reheat gently and serve over the rice.

GRITS

66. Grits and Grillades

MAKES 6 SERVINGS

1 (3-pound) beef or veal round steak, pounded to about 1/4 inch thick
Salt and freshly ground black pepper, to taste
1 cup all-purpose flour
¾ cup vegetable oil, divided
1 large onion, chopped
1 green bell pepper, chopped
1 bunch green onions, chopped, green and white parts separated
3 garlic cloves, minced
1 large tomato, chopped
1 tablespoon tomato paste
½ cup red wine
3 cups water
1 teaspoon red wine vinegar
½ teaspoon dried thyme
1 tablespoon Worcestershire sauce
Salt, freshly ground black pepper, and Creole seasoning, to taste
3 tablespoons chopped flat-leaf parsley
Grits to serve 6, cooked according to package

INSTRUCTIONS:

Cut the beef into roughly 2 × 3-inch pieces. Season both sides liberally with salt and pepper.

Heat 1/4 cup of the oil in a large, heavy skillet and place the flour in a shallow bowl or plate. Dredge each piece of steak in the flour, shake off the excess, and brown on both sides. Transfer the meat to paper towels.

Add the remaining oil to the skillet and sauté the onions, the white parts of the green onions, the bell pepper, and the garlic until translucent. Add the tomato, tomato paste, wine, water, vinegar, thyme, Worcestershire sauce, and meat and season with salt, pepper, and Creole seasoning. Bring to a boil. Reduce the heat, cover, and simmer until the meat is tender, about 1 ½ hours. Add the parsley and green onion tops and serve over the grits.

67. Shrimp and Grits

MAKES 6 SERVINGS

INGREDIENTS:
- 3 pounds large shrimp (about 15 to 20 to the pound), peeled and deveined
- 5 tablespoons butter, divided
- 8 green onions, chopped
- 5 large garlic cloves, minced
- Zest and juice of 1 lemon
- 1/3 cup dry white wine
- 1 tablespoon Worcestershire sauce
- 1 teaspoon Italian seasoning
- Freshly ground black pepper, to taste
- ½ teaspoon plus 1/4 teaspoon salt, divided
- 1 teaspoon Creole seasoning
- 2 tablespoons chopped flat-leaf parsley
- 1 cup quick grits
- 4 1/4 cups water
- 1/4 cup freshly grated Parmesan

INSTRUCTIONS:
a) Melt 4 tablespoons of the butter in a large, heavy skillet over medium heat. Add the onions and garlic and sauté until wilted. Add the shrimp and sauté, stirring, for a few minutes until they turn pink. Add the lemon zest and juice, wine, Worcestershire sauce, Italian seasoning, pepper, Creole seasoning, and ½ teaspoon of the salt and simmer for about 3 minutes. Do not overcook the shrimp. Remove from the heat and sprinkle with parsley.

b) To cook the grits, bring the water to a boil in a large saucepan and add the grits in a steady stream while stirring. Add the remaining salt. Cover, reduce the heat to low, and simmer for about 10 minutes. Remove from the heat and stir in the Parmesan and remaining butter. Serve the shrimp over the grits on plates or in bowls.

68. Shrimp, Andouille Sausage, and Grits

Makes: 4 Servings

INGREDIENTS

3 cups water
2 teaspoons kosher salt
¾ cup quick grits
2 tablespoons extra-virgin olive oil
½ pound andouille sausage, cut into ½-inch-thick slices
½ pound large raw shrimp, peeled and deveined
1 teaspoon minced garlic
¼ cup chopped green onions, plus more for garnish
2 teaspoons Cajun seasoning
½ teaspoon ground black pepper
3 tablespoons salted butter

INSTRUCTIONS

In a medium saucepan over high heat, pour in the water and salt. Once the liquid starts to boil, immediately turn the heat down to medium. Stir the liquid, and gradually sprinkle in the grits. Let the grits cook until they thicken and get nice and creamy (usually 30 to 35 minutes), and be sure to stir frequently.

While the grits are cooking, grab a pan and drizzle in the olive oil. Heat the oil up over medium-high heat, then toss in the andouille sausage. Cook for 5 to 7 minutes, or until it browns, then toss in the shrimp, garlic, and green onions. Sprinkle in the Cajun seasoning and black pepper.

Cook for 5 more minutes, then turn off the heat. Once the grits have thickened, add in the butter and stir.

Plate the grits, then add the sausage, shrimp, and onions on top. Garnish with extra green onions.

69. **Creamy Cheesy Grits**

Makes: 4 TO 6 Servings

INGREDIENTS
3 cups water
½ cup heavy cream
1 cup quick grits
4 tablespoons salted butter
1 teaspoon kosher salt
½ teaspoon ground black pepper
½ cup shredded creamy Havarti cheese
½ cup shredded sharp cheddar cheese

INSTRUCTIONS
In a medium saucepan over high heat, pour in the water and heavy cream. Once it reaches a full boil, sprinkle in the grits and whisk. Reduce the heat to medium low and cook for 30 to 35 minutes, stirring occasionally to prevent lumps.
Add the butter, and sprinkle in the salt, pepper, and cheese. Stir until everything is nice and creamy and well combined. Turn the heat off, then serve with your favorite breakfast dishes.

70. Hominy souffle

Makes: 8 servings

INGREDIENTS:
1 cup Milk
1 cup Water
½ cup Hominy grits
2 tablespoons Butter, melted
¾ teaspoon Salt
3 Egg, separated, well beaten

1. Scald milk and water in the top of a double boiler.

2. Add hominy grits, stirring until thickened; cook 1 hour.

3. Cool; add butter, salt and egg yolks, blending well.

4. Gently fold in stiffly beaten egg whites.

Pour mixture into a well-buttered casserole; bake in preheated 325'F. oven 45 minutes.

71. Goat cheese polenta with sun dried tomatoes

Makes: 4 Servings

INGREDIENTS:
- 1 cup Plus 2 tablespoons yellow Corn grits
- 2 (14 1/2-ounce) cans fat-free Chicken stock
- 2 Garlic cloves, pressed or Minced
- 6 ounces Goat cheese, crumbled
- ½ cup Sun-dried tomatoes, cut into Matchstick-size strips

INSTRUCTIONS:

a) Combine grits, chicken stock and garlic in large saucepan with tight-fitting lid.

b) Bring to boil over medium heat, stirring frequently.

c) Reduce heat to low and cook, stirring occasionally, for 20 minutes. Remove from heat and stir in goat cheese and sun-dried tomatoes.

d) Spray a baking dish with nonstick cooking spray.

e) Spoon grits mixture into dish and press with wet hands to spread evenly.

f) Cool to room temperature and refrigerate.

g) When well chilled, turn out onto cutting board and cut into 64 squares to serve as hors d'oeuvres.

FRIED CATFISH

72. Classic Southern Fried Catfish

Ingredients:

4-6 catfish fillets
1 cup all-purpose flour
1 tsp salt
1/2 tsp black pepper
1/4 tsp cayenne pepper
1/4 tsp garlic powder
1/4 tsp onion powder
1/4 tsp paprika
1 cup buttermilk
Vegetable oil, for frying
Instructions:

In a shallow bowl, mix together the flour, salt, black pepper, cayenne pepper, garlic powder, onion powder, and paprika.

In another shallow bowl, pour the buttermilk.

Dip each catfish fillet in the buttermilk, then coat it in the flour mixture, shaking off any excess.

Heat about 1 inch of vegetable oil in a large skillet over medium-high heat.

Fry the catfish fillets in batches until golden brown and cooked through, about 3-4 minutes per side. Drain them on paper towels.

73. Cajun Blackened Catfish

Ingredients:

4-6 catfish fillets
1/4 cup melted butter
1 tbsp paprika
1 tsp garlic powder
1 tsp onion powder
1 tsp salt
1/2 tsp black pepper
1/2 tsp cayenne pepper
Vegetable oil, for frying

Instructions:

In a small bowl, mix together the paprika, garlic powder, onion powder, salt, black pepper, and cayenne pepper.

Brush each catfish fillet with melted butter, then coat both sides with the spice mixture.

Heat about 1/4 inch of vegetable oil in a large skillet over high heat.

Add the catfish fillets and cook for about 3-4 minutes per side, until blackened and cooked through.

74. Cornmeal-Crusted Fried Catfish

Ingredients:

4-6 catfish fillets
1/2 cup all-purpose flour
1/2 cup yellow cornmeal
1 tsp salt
1/2 tsp black pepper
1/2 tsp cayenne pepper
1/4 tsp garlic powder
1/4 tsp onion powder
1/4 tsp paprika
1 cup buttermilk
Vegetable oil, for frying

Instructions:

In a shallow bowl, mix together the flour, cornmeal, salt, black pepper, cayenne pepper, garlic powder, onion powder, and paprika.

In another shallow bowl, pour the buttermilk.

Dip each catfish fillet in the buttermilk, then coat it in the flour mixture, shaking off any excess.

Heat about 1 inch of vegetable oil in a large skillet over medium-high heat.

Fry the catfish fillets in batches until golden brown and cooked through, about 3-4 minutes per side. Drain them on paper towels.

75. Panko-Crusted Fried Catfish

Ingredients:

4-6 catfish fillets
1 cup all-purpose flour
1 tsp salt
1/2 tsp black pepper
1/4 tsp cayenne pepper
1 cup buttermilk
1 cup panko breadcrumbs
Vegetable oil, for frying

Instructions:

In a shallow bowl, mix together the flour, salt, black pepper, and cayenne pepper.
In another shallow bowl, pour the buttermilk.
3. Dip each catfish fillet in the buttermilk, then coat it in the flour mixture, shaking off any excess.

Dip the floured fillets into the panko breadcrumbs, pressing them gently to adhere.

Heat about 1 inch of vegetable oil in a large skillet over medium-high heat.

Fry the catfish fillets in batches until golden brown and cooked through, about 3-4 minutes per side. Drain them on paper towels.

76. Lemon-Pepper Fried Catfish

Ingredients:

4-6 catfish fillets
1 cup all-purpose flour
1 tsp salt
1 tsp lemon pepper seasoning
1/2 tsp garlic powder
1/2 tsp onion powder
1/2 tsp paprika
1 cup buttermilk
Vegetable oil, for frying

Instructions:

In a shallow bowl, mix together the flour, salt, lemon pepper seasoning, garlic powder, onion powder, and paprika.

In another shallow bowl, pour the buttermilk.

Dip each catfish fillet in the buttermilk, then coat it in the flour mixture, shaking off any excess.

Heat about 1 inch of vegetable oil in a large skillet over medium-high heat.

Fry the catfish fillets in batches until golden brown and cooked through, about 3-4 minutes per side. Drain them on paper towels.

77. Buttermilk and Hot Sauce Fried Catfish

Ingredients:

4-6 catfish fillets
1 cup all-purpose flour
1 tsp salt
1/2 tsp black pepper
1/4 tsp cayenne pepper
1/4 tsp garlic powder
1/4 tsp onion powder
1/4 tsp paprika
1 cup buttermilk
2 tbsp hot sauce
Vegetable oil, for frying

Instructions:

In a shallow bowl, mix together the flour, salt, black pepper, cayenne pepper, garlic powder, onion powder, and paprika.
In another shallow bowl, pour the buttermilk and hot sauce.
Dip each catfish fillet in the buttermilk mixture, then coat it in the flour mixture, shaking off any excess.
Heat about 1 inch of vegetable oil in a large skillet over medium-high heat.
Fry the catfish fillets in batches until golden brown and cooked through, about 3-4 minutes per side. Drain them on paper towels.

BOUDIN BALLS

78. Classic Boudin Balls

Ingredients:

1 lb. pork or chicken boudin
1/2 cup all-purpose flour
2 eggs, beaten
1 cup breadcrumbs
Salt and black pepper, to taste
Vegetable oil, for frying
Instructions:

Preheat the oven to 350°F.

Roll the boudin into small balls, about 1-2 inches in diameter.

Dredge the balls in the flour, then dip them in the beaten eggs, and roll them in the breadcrumbs to coat.

Heat about 1 inch of vegetable oil in a large skillet over medium-high heat.

Fry the boudin balls in batches until golden brown and crispy, about 2-3 minutes per batch. Drain them on paper towels.

Transfer the fried boudin balls to a baking sheet and bake in the preheated oven for 5-10 minutes to ensure they are fully cooked through.

79. Spicy Boudin Balls

Ingredients:

1 lb. pork or chicken boudin
1 jalapeño pepper, seeded and finely chopped
1/4 cup chopped green onions
1/4 cup chopped fresh parsley
1/2 cup all-purpose flour
2 eggs, beaten
1 cup seasoned breadcrumbs
Salt and black pepper, to taste
Vegetable oil, for frying

Instructions:

In a large bowl, mix together the boudin, jalapeño pepper, green onions, and parsley.

Roll the mixture into small balls, about 1-2 inches in diameter.

Dredge the balls in the flour, then dip them in the beaten eggs, and roll them in the seasoned breadcrumbs to coat.

Heat about 1 inch of vegetable oil in a large skillet over medium-high heat.

Fry the boudin balls in batches until golden brown and crispy, about 2-3 minutes per batch. Drain them on paper towels.

80. Cheese-Stuffed Boudin Balls

Ingredients:

1 lb. pork or chicken boudin
4 oz. cream cheese, softened
1/4 cup grated Parmesan cheese
1/4 cup chopped green onions
1/2 cup all-purpose flour
2 eggs, beaten
1 cup seasoned breadcrumbs
Salt and black pepper, to taste
Vegetable oil, for frying
Instructions:

In a large bowl, mix together the boudin, cream cheese, Parmesan cheese, and green onions.

Roll the mixture into small balls, about 1-2 inches in diameter.

Dredge the balls in the flour, then flatten them slightly and place a small cube of cheese in the center. Roll the balls around the cheese to cover it completely.

Dip the balls in the beaten eggs, and roll them in the seasoned breadcrumbs to coat.

Heat about 1 inch of vegetable oil in a large skillet over medium-high heat.

Fry the boudin balls in batches until golden brown and crispy, about 2-3 minutes per batch. Drain them on paper towels.

81. Crawfish Boudin Balls

Ingredients:

1 lb. crawfish boudin
1/4 cup chopped green onions
1/4 cup chopped fresh parsley
1/2 cup all-purpose flour
2 eggs, beaten
1 cup seasoned breadcrumbs
Salt and black pepper, to taste
Vegetable oil

Instructions:

In a large bowl, mix together the crawfish boudin, green onions, and parsley.

Roll the mixture into small balls, about 1-2 inches in diameter.

Dredge the balls in the flour, then dip them in the beaten eggs, and roll them in the seasoned breadcrumbs to coat.

Heat about 1 inch of vegetable oil in a large skillet over medium-high heat.

Fry the crawfish boudin balls in batches until golden brown and crispy, about 2-3 minutes per batch. Drain them on paper towels.

82. Smoked Boudin Balls

Ingredients:

1 lb. smoked boudin
1/4 cup chopped green onions
1/4 cup chopped fresh parsley
1/2 cup all-purpose flour
2 eggs, beaten
1 cup seasoned breadcrumbs
Salt and black pepper, to taste
Vegetable oil, for frying
Instructions:

In a large bowl, mix together the smoked boudin, green onions, and parsley.
Roll the mixture into small balls, about 1-2 inches in diameter.
Dredge the balls in the flour, then dip them in the beaten eggs, and roll them in the seasoned breadcrumbs to coat.
Heat about 1 inch of vegetable oil in a large skillet over medium-high heat.
Fry the smoked boudin balls in batches until golden brown and crispy, about 2-3 minutes per batch. Drain them on paper towels.

PO' BOYS

83. Shrimp Po' Boy

Ingredients:

1 lb. medium shrimp, peeled and deveined
1 cup buttermilk
1 cup all-purpose flour
1 tsp. garlic powder
1 tsp. paprika
1/2 tsp. cayenne pepper
Salt and black pepper, to taste
Vegetable oil, for frying
French bread rolls
Lettuce, sliced tomatoes, and mayonnaise, for serving

Instructions:

In a large bowl, combine the shrimp and buttermilk, and stir to coat the shrimp. Cover the bowl and refrigerate for 1 hour.

In a shallow dish, combine the flour, garlic powder, paprika, cayenne pepper, salt, and black pepper, and stir to combine.

In a large skillet, heat about 1 inch of vegetable oil over medium-high heat. Dredge the shrimp in the flour mixture, shaking off any excess, and fry in batches until golden brown and crispy, about 2-3 minutes per batch. Drain the shrimp on paper towels.

Slice the French bread rolls in half lengthwise, and spread mayonnaise on both sides. Add lettuce and sliced tomatoes, then top with the fried shrimp. Serve hot.

84. Oyster Po' Boy

Ingredients:

1 pint fresh oysters, shucked
1 cup all-purpose flour
1 tsp. garlic powder
1 tsp. paprika
1/2 tsp. cayenne pepper
Salt and black pepper, to taste
Vegetable oil, for frying
French bread rolls
Lettuce, sliced tomatoes, and mayonnaise, for serving

Instructions:

In a shallow dish, combine the flour, garlic powder, paprika, cayenne pepper, salt, and black pepper, and stir to combine.

In a large skillet, heat about 1 inch of vegetable oil over medium-high heat. Dredge the oysters in the flour mixture, shaking off any excess, and fry in batches until golden brown and crispy, about 2-3 minutes per batch. Drain the oysters on paper towels.

Slice the French bread rolls in half lengthwise, and spread mayonnaise on both sides. Add lettuce and sliced tomatoes, then top with the fried oysters. Serve hot.

85. **Fried Chicken Po' Boy**

Ingredients:

2 boneless, skinless chicken breasts, cut into thin strips
1 cup all-purpose flour
1 tsp. paprika
1 tsp. garlic powder
1/2 tsp. cayenne pepper
Salt and black pepper, to taste
1/2 cup buttermilk
Vegetable oil, for frying
French bread rolls
Lettuce, sliced tomatoes, and mayonnaise, for serving

Instructions:

In a shallow dish, combine the flour, paprika, garlic powder, cayenne pepper, salt, and black pepper, and stir to combine.
In a separate dish, pour the buttermilk.
Heat about 1 inch of vegetable oil in a large skillet over medium-high heat.
Dredge the chicken strips in the flour mixture, shaking off any excess, and then dip them in the buttermilk. Dredge them in the flour mixture again to coat.
Fry the chicken strips in batches in the hot oil until golden brown and crispy, about 3-4 minutes per batch. Drain the chicken on paper towels.
Slice the French bread rolls in half lengthwise, and spread mayonnaise on both sides. Add lettuce and sliced tomatoes, then top with the fried chicken. Serve hot.

86. Catfish Po' Boy

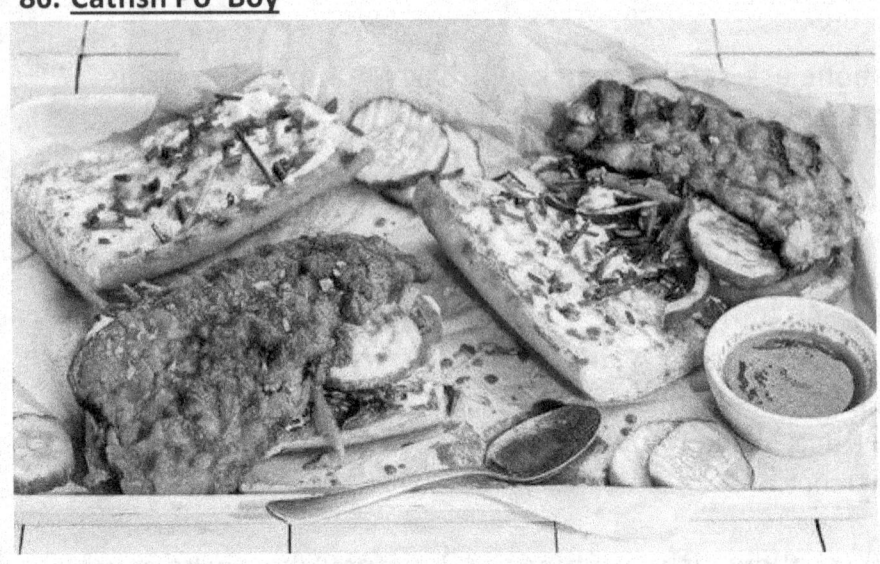

Ingredients:

1 lb. catfish fillets, cut into strips
1 cup buttermilk
1 cup cornmeal
1 tsp. garlic powder
1 tsp. paprika
1/2 tsp. cayenne pepper
Salt and black pepper, to taste
Vegetable oil, for frying
French bread rolls
Lettuce, sliced tomatoes, and mayonnaise, for serving

Instructions:

In a large bowl, combine the catfish and buttermilk, and stir to coat the fish. Cover the bowl and refrigerate for 1 hour.

In a shallow dish, combine the cornmeal, garlic powder, paprika, cayenne pepper, salt, and black pepper, and stir to combine.

In a large skillet, heat about 1 inch of vegetable oil over medium-high heat. Dredge the catfish in the cornmeal mixture, shaking off any excess, and fry in batches until golden brown and crispy, about 2-3 minutes per batch. Drain the catfish on paper towels.

Slice the French bread rolls in half lengthwise, and spread mayonnaise on both sides. Add lettuce and sliced tomatoes, then top with the fried catfish. Serve hot.

87. Roast Beef Po' Boy

Ingredients:

1 lb. deli roast beef, thinly sliced
1/2 cup mayonnaise
2 tbsp. horseradish
2 tbsp. ketchup
1 tbsp. Worcestershire sauce
Salt and black pepper, to taste
French bread rolls
Lettuce, sliced tomatoes, and pickles, for serving
Instructions:

In a small bowl, whisk together the mayonnaise, horseradish, ketchup, Worcestershire sauce, salt, and black pepper.
Slice the French bread rolls in half lengthwise, and spread the mayonnaise mixture on both sides.
Add the roast beef, lettuce, sliced tomatoes, and pickles to the rolls, and serve immediately.

REDFISH COURTBOUILLON

88. Louisiana Redfish Courtbouillon

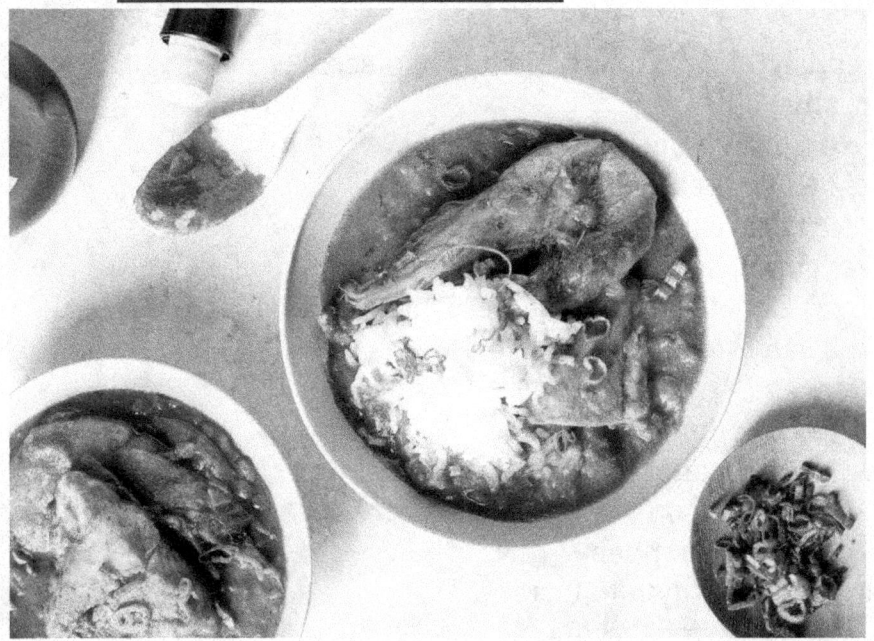

Ingredients:

2 lb. redfish fillets, cut into bite-sized pieces
2 tbsp. olive oil
1 large onion, chopped
1 large bell pepper, chopped
2 celery stalks, chopped
2 cloves garlic, minced
1 (28-oz.) can whole tomatoes, crushed by hand
1 (8-oz.) can tomato sauce
2 bay leaves
1 tsp. dried thyme
1 tsp. dried oregano
1 tsp. paprika
1/2 tsp. cayenne pepper
Salt and black pepper, to taste
Hot cooked rice, for serving

Instructions:

In a large Dutch oven or heavy pot, heat the olive oil over medium heat. Add the onion, bell pepper, celery, and garlic, and cook until the vegetables are softened, about 5 minutes.

Add the crushed tomatoes, tomato sauce, bay leaves, thyme, oregano, paprika, cayenne pepper, salt, and black pepper to the pot. Bring the mixture to a simmer, then reduce the heat to low and cook for 30 minutes.

Add the redfish to the pot and cook for an additional 10-15 minutes, until the fish is cooked through and flakes easily with a fork.

Serve the courtbouillon hot over hot cooked rice.

89. Emeril Lagasse Redfish Courtbouillon

Ingredients:

4 tbsp. vegetable oil
2 lb. redfish fillets, cut into bite-sized pieces
1 large onion, chopped
1 large bell pepper, chopped
3 celery stalks, chopped
4 cloves garlic, minced
1 (28-oz.) can whole tomatoes, crushed by hand
2 bay leaves
1 tsp. dried thyme
1 tsp. dried oregano
1 tsp. paprika
1/4 tsp. cayenne pepper
Salt and black pepper, to taste
4 cups cooked white rice, for serving

Instructions:

In a large Dutch oven or heavy pot, heat the vegetable oil over medium-high heat. Add the redfish and cook for 2-3 minutes on each side, until lightly browned. Remove the fish from the pot and set it aside.

Add the onion, bell pepper, celery, and garlic to the pot, and cook for 5-7 minutes, until the vegetables are softened.

Add the crushed tomatoes, bay leaves, thyme, oregano, paprika, cayenne pepper, salt, and black pepper to the pot. Bring the mixture to a simmer, then reduce the heat to low and cook for 15-20 minutes.

Add the redfish to the pot and cook for an additional 10-15 minutes, until the fish is cooked through and flakes easily with a fork.

Serve the courtbouillon hot over cooked white rice.

90. Saveur Redfish Courtbouillon

Ingredients:

1/4 cup vegetable oil
2 lb. redfish fillets, cut into bite-sized pieces
1 large onion, chopped
1 large bell pepper, chopped
2 celery stalks, chopped
2 cloves garlic, minced
1 (14-oz.) can diced tomatoes, drained
1 (8-oz.) can tomato sauce
1 tsp. paprika
1/2 tsp. cayenne pepper
1 tsp. dried thyme
1 tsp. dried oregano
Salt and black pepper, to taste
4 cups cooked white rice, for serving

Instructions:

In a large Dutch oven or heavy pot, heat the vegetable oil over medium-high heat. Add the redfish and cook for 2-3 minutes on each side, until lightly browned. Remove the fish from the pot and set it aside.

Add the onion, bell pepper, celery, and garlic to the pot, and cook for 5-7 minutes, until the vegetables are softened.

Add the diced tomatoes, tomato sauce, paprika, cayenne pepper, thyme, oregano, salt, and black pepper to the pot, and stir to combine. Bring the mixture to a simmer, then reduce the heat to low and cook for 15-20 minutes.

Add the redfish to the pot and cook for an additional 10-15 minutes, until the fish is cooked through and flakes easily with a fork.

Serve the courtbouillon hot over cooked white rice.

BEIGNETS

91. Grand Marnier beignets

Ingredients
- 1 package dry yeast
- 4 tablespoons warm water
- 3 ½ cups flour
- 1 teaspoon salt
- ¼ cup sugar
- 1 teaspoon orange granules
- 1 ⅛ cups milk
- 3 eggs, beaten
- ¼ cup melted butter
- ⅛ cup Grand Marnier
- 1 cup powdered sugar
- ¼ cup lemon juice (optional)
- oil for deep-frying

Directions
1. In a small bowl, dissolve the yeast in the warm water. Set bowl aside in a warm place for 15–20 minutes.
2. Heat the oil in a deep fryer to 375°F. In a large mixing bowl, combine the flour, salt, sugar, and orange granules, and mix well to ensure proper blending. Fold in the dissolved yeast, the milk, eggs, butter, and liqueur. Continue to blend until a smooth beignet dough is formed. Place the dough in a medium metal bowl, cover with a damp towel, and allow the dough to rise for one hour.
3. Remove the dough to a well-floured surface and roll out to approximately 1/4" thickness. Cut it into rectangular shapes, 2"x 3", and return them to a lightly floured pan. Cover the pan with a towel and allow the dough to rise for 35 to 45 minutes.

4. Deep fry the squares in the hot oil, turning once, until golden brown, about 3-4 minutes. Remove from the oil with a slotted spoon or basket strainer. Drain Beignets on a paper towel, and then dust generously with powdered sugar. You can also sprinkle with fresh lemon juice.
5. Serve warm with chicory coffee or other strong blend.
6. Serves 8-10

92. Beignets with cinnamon sugar

MAKES ABOUT 28 BEIGNETS

350ml warm water

170ml evaporated milk
2 eggs
50g butter, softened
900g plain flour
100g caster sugar

1 teaspoon fast-action yeast a pinch of salt vegetable oil, for greasing 100g icing sugar

1 teaspoon ground cinnamon, or to taste

Place the water, evaporated milk, eggs and butter in the bowl of a food mixer and beat gently with the paddle attachment until combined. Add the flour, sugar, yeast and salt and continue to beat gently until well mixed in. Increase the speed and beat for another 3–4 minutes until you get a smooth, sticky dough. I would not advise making this dough by hand, as it is a wet and sticky dough and much easier made using a food mixer.

Lightly oil a large bowl and scrape the dough into it, turning it once or twice so it has a thin coating of oil all over. Cover the bowl with cling film (the oiled surface will prevent it from sticking should it rise that high) and set aside to prove for 3–4 hours on the worktop; it should double in size. You could also prove the dough in the fridge overnight.

Sift the icing sugar into a bowl and stir through the cinnamon. Set aside.

Turn out the ball of dough on to a lightly oiled worktop and slice into quarters. Roll each piece into a sausage shape of about 3cm diameter and cut on the diagonal into 2–3cm slices – you should get about 7 beignets from each quarter. If you wish to freeze a batch, space them out on a baking tray to freeze initially, then pack into a bag or tub and leave in the freezer until you want to eat (they cook from frozen so no need to defrost).

Heat the oil in a deep fat fryer to 180°C/350°F. Add about 4 or 5 beignets at a time and fry for 4 minutes until deep golden brown, carefully turning halfway with a fork to cook the other side. If cooking from frozen, add an extra minute or two to the cooking time. Drain for a few moments on kitchen paper before tossing in the cinnamon-flavoured icing sugar and setting aside on a plate. Repeat with the remaining beignets. Serve immediately while still hot.

LAGNIAPPE

93. Lagniappe

MAKES 6–8 SERVINGS

INGREDIENTS:
- 2 pounds boneless, trimmed alligator, cut into 1-inch pieces
- Salt and freshly ground black pepper, to taste
- 2 tablespoons plus ½ cup vegetable oil, divided
- 3/4 cup all-purpose flour
- 1 large onion, chopped
- 1 bunch green onions, chopped, white and green parts separated
- 1 green bell pepper, chopped
- 2 celery stalks, chopped
- 4 garlic cloves, minced
- 2 large fresh tomatoes, in season, peeled and chopped, or 1 (14-ounce) can chopped plum tomatoes
- 1 (10-ounce) can original Ro-tel tomatoes
- Juice of 1 lemon
- 2 tablespoons Worcestershire sauce
- 1 teaspoon salt
- ½ teaspoon freshly ground black pepper
- 1/4 teaspoon cayenne pepper
- 2 bay leaves
- 2 cups beef stock
- 1/3 cup chopped flat-leaf parsley
- Cooked long-grain white rice, for serving

INSTRUCTIONS:

a) Season the alligator with salt and pepper. Heat 2 tablespoons of the oil in a large skillet, add the alligator pieces, and sear on all sides. The meat will not turn brown. Remove the alligator and set aside. Save the pan for later deglazing.

b) Heat the remaining oil in a large, heavy pot over medium-high heat; add the flour and stir constantly until the roux begins to brown. Reduce the heat to medium and cook, stirring constantly, until the roux turns a reddish-brown color. Immediately add the onion, the white parts of the green onions, the bell peppers, and the celery and sauté over medium-low heat until translucent. Add the garlic and sauté a minute more. Return the alligator to the pot.

c) Meanwhile, heat a little of the stock in the skillet over high heat to deglaze. Stir the liquid, being sure to scrape up the brown bits from the bottom of the skillet, and add this to the pot.

d) Add the rest of the ingredients except the parsley to the pot. Cover and simmer over low heat, stirring occasionally, until the meat is tender, about 30 minutes. Adjust the seasonings, add the green onion tops and parsley, and remove the bay leaves. Serve over the hot rice.

94. Calas

MAKES 30 CALAS

INGREDIENTS:
- ½ cup all-purpose flour
- 2 ½ teaspoons baking powder
- 1/3 cup sugar
- ½ teaspoon salt
- ½ teaspoon freshly grated nutmeg
- 3 eggs
- 1 teaspoon vanilla
- 2 cups cooked long-grain white rice
- Vegetable oil for deep frying
- Confectioners' sugar to sprinkle

INSTRUCTIONS:
a) In a large bowl, whisk together the flour, baking powder, sugar, salt, and nutmeg. Add the eggs and vanilla and mix well. Stir in the rice.
b) In a large frying pan or deep fryer, heat the oil to 360°. Carefully drop the mixture by teaspoonfuls into the hot oil in batches. Fry the dough, turning often, until golden brown, and remove to paper towels.
c) Sprinkle with confectioners' sugar and serve hot.

95. Corn Maque Choux

MAKES 8 SERVINGS

INGREDIENTS:
- 6–8 ears yellow corn
- 2 tablespoons butter
- 1 green bell pepper, chopped
- 1 medium onion, chopped
- 1 large tomato, chopped
- 2 garlic cloves, minced
- 3/4 cup water
- Pinch cayenne pepper
- 1 teaspoon sugar
- Salt and freshly ground black pepper, to taste

INSTRUCTIONS:
a) Rinse and clear the corn of silks. Using a very sharp knife over a wide bowl, cut through the kernels halfway to the cob. Use a table knife to scrape the juices from the remaining part of kernels. Set aside.

b) In a large, heavy skillet or medium pot, heat the butter and sauté the bell pepper and onion until translucent. Add the tomato and garlic and cook over medium heat for 5 minutes. Add the water, corn, cayenne pepper, and sugar and season with salt and pepper. Bring to a boil, reduce heat to low, cover, and simmer until corn is done, about 30 minutes. Taste and adjust seasonings.

96. Crawfish Bisque

MAKES 4 SERVINGS

INGREDIENTS:
- 3 tablespoons plus ½ cup vegetable oil, divided
- 2 pounds fresh crawfish tails, thawed, divided
- 1 onion, chopped and divided
- 1 bunch green onions, chopped and divided
- 1 green bell pepper, chopped and divided
- 3 garlic cloves, minced and divided
- 3/4 teaspoon salt, divided
- 3/4 teaspoon freshly ground black pepper, divided
- 3/4 teaspoon Creole seasoning, divided
- 2 cups bread crumbs1 egg, beaten
- 2/3 cup plus ½ cup all-purpose flour, divided
- 5 cups seafood stock or water
- 2 tablespoons tomato paste
- Pinch cayenne pepper, or to taste
- 2 cups cooked long-grain white rice
- 2 tablespoons chopped flat-leaf parsley

INSTRUCTIONS:
a) Heat the oven to 350°. Spray a large baking sheet with nonstick cooking spray and set aside.
b) Heat 3 tablespoons of the oil in a large skillet and sauté half the onions, green onions, bell pepper, and garlic. Add 1 pound of the crawfish and sauté for 5 minutes. Remove the mixture to a food processor and grind to the consistency of ground meat. Transfer the mixture to a bowl and add 1/4 teaspoon of the salt, 1/4 teaspoon of the pepper, 1/4 teaspoon of the Creole seasoning, the bread crumbs, and the egg and combine well.
c) Place 2/3 cup of the flour in a shallow baking dish. Roll the mixture into 1-inch balls. Roll the balls in the flour and place them on the baking sheet. Bake, turning the balls several times, until lightly browned all over, about 35 minutes. Set aside.

d) Heat the remaining oil in a medium, heavy pot over medium-high heat. Add the remaining flour, stirring constantly, until it turns a peanut butter color. Add the remaining onions, bell pepper, and garlic, and cook until translucent. Add the stock or water, tomato paste, the remaining salt, pepper, and Creole seasoning, and the cayenne pepper, and simmer, covered, for 15 minutes.

e) Mince the remaining crawfish tails and add to the bisque and continue cooking for 15 minutes. For a smooth bisque, blend with a hand blender. Add the crawfish balls and simmer for 5 more minutes.

f) Serve in bowls over the rice. Sprinkle with parsley.

97. Crawfish Étouffée

MAKES 8–10 SERVINGS

INGREDIENTS:
- 3/4 cup butter or vegetable oil
- 3/4 cup all-purpose flour
- 1 large onion, chopped
- 1 bunch green onions, chopped, white and green parts separated
- 1 green bell pepper, chopped
- 3 celery stalks, chopped.
- 4 large garlic cloves, minced
- 3 tablespoons tomato paste
- 6 cups seafood stock or water
- ½ teaspoon dried thyme
- 3 bay leaves
- 1 teaspoon Creole seasoning
- 1 teaspoon salt
- 1 tablespoon fresh lemon juice
- Cayenne pepper and freshly ground black pepper, to taste
- 2–3 pounds crawfish tails with fat
- 3 tablespoons chopped flat-leaf parsley
- Cooked long-grain white rice, for serving

INSTRUCTIONS:

d) In a large, heavy pot, melt the butter or heat the oil over medium heat. Add the flour and stir constantly. If using butter, cook the roux until it turns a blonde or golden color. If using oil, continue cooking, stirring, until the roux is medium brown. Add the onions, the white parts of the green onions, the bell peppers, the celery, and the garlic and sauté, stirring, until translucent.

e) Add the tomato paste, stock or water, thyme, bay leaves, Creole seasoning, salt, and lemon juice, season with the cayenne and pepper, and bring to a boil. Reduce the heat, cover, and simmer for 20 minutes, stirring occasionally and skimming any fat off the top. Add the crawfish, parsley, and green onion tops, bring to a boil, reduce the heat, and simmer for 10 minutes. Remove the bay leaves.

f) When ready to serve, reheat gently and serve over the rice.

98. Crawfish Pies

MAKES 5 (5-INCH) INDIVIDUAL PIES

INGREDIENTS:
- Enough dough for four 9-inch pies (store-bought is fine)
- 2 pounds crawfish tails with fat, divided
- 6 tablespoons butter
- 6 tablespoons all-purpose flour
- 2 medium onions, chopped
- 1 green bell pepper, chopped
- 4 garlic cloves, minced
- 2 cups half-and-half
- 4 tablespoons sherry
- 2 tablespoons fresh lemon juice
- 1 teaspoon salt
- 15 turns on a black pepper mill
- 1 teaspoon cayenne pepper
- 4 tablespoons chopped flat-leaf parsley
- 1 egg white, beaten

INSTRUCTIONS:
a) Preheat the oven to 350°.
b) Roll out the pie dough to 1/8-inch thickness. You should have
c) enough dough for five 5-inch double-crusted pies. To get the right size for the bottom crusts, place one of the pans upside-down on the dough and cut the dough 1 inch from the edge of the pan. The top crusts should be cut at 5 inches for the best fit. Place the bottom crusts into the pie pans and keep the top crusts cold in the refrigerator.
d) In a food processor, chop half the crawfish tails until nearly ground. Leave the others whole.
e) Melt the butter in a medium, heavy pot or large skillet over medium heat. Add the flour and stir constantly until the roux is light brown. Add the onion and bell pepper and sauté for about 5 minutes. Add the garlic and sauté 1 minute more. Add the half-and-half, sherry, lemon juice, salt, pepper, cayenne, and parsley and cook for 5 minutes. Add the chopped and whole crawfish and cook 5 minutes more.
f) Fill each of the prepared pie shells with about 1 cup of the crawfish filling. Cover with the top crusts and crimp the edges. Cut several slits in the top crust and brush with the egg white. Place the pies on cookie sheets and bake until the filling is bubbly and the crusts are golden brown, about 1 hour.

99. Dirty Rice

MAKES 8–10 SERVINGS

INGREDIENTS:
- 3 cups water
- 1 ½ cups long-grain white rice
- 1/4 plus 1 teaspoon salt, divided
- 2 tablespoons vegetable oil
- 1 onion, chopped
- 6 green onions, chopped, white and green parts separated
- 1 green bell pepper, chopped
- 2 celery stalks, chopped
- 3 garlic cloves, minced
- 1 pound ground beef
- 1 pound chicken livers, chopped
- ½ teaspoon freshly ground black pepper
- ½ teaspoon cayenne pepper
- 1/3 cup chopped flat-leaf parsley

INSTRUCTIONS:
a) Bring the water to boil in a medium saucepan. Add the rice and 1/4 teaspoon of the salt. Reduce the heat to low, cover, and cook until all the water has been absorbed, about 20 minutes.
b) In a medium, heavy pot, heat the oil and sauté the onion, the white parts of the green onions, the bell pepper, and the celery until translucent. Add the garlic and sauté a minute more. Add the ground beef and brown, stirring. Add the chicken livers and continue cooking and stirring until the beef and livers are cooked through, about 10 minutes. Add the pepper and cayenne, cover, and simmer for 5 minutes.
c) Stir in the parsley and green onion tops. Gently fold in the rice. Serve with Louisiana hot sauce on the side.

100. Eggs Sardou

MAKES 4 SERVINGS

INGREDIENTS:
FOR THE HOLLANDAISE SAUCE
- 2 large egg yolks
- 1 ½ tablespoons fresh lemon juice
- 2 sticks unsalted butter
- Salt and freshly ground black pepper, to taste

FOR THE EGGS
- 2 (9-ounce) bags fresh spinach
- 1 tablespoon olive oil
- 1 teaspoon minced garlic
- 1/3 cup heavy cream
- Salt and freshly ground black pepper, to taste
- 8 fresh-cooked or canned artichoke bottoms
- 2 tablespoons white vinegar
- 8 eggs

INSTRUCTIONS:

a) To make the sauce, place the egg yolks and lemon juice in a blender. Pulse several times to mix.

b) Melt the butter in a glass pitcher in the microwave, being careful not to boil it. Gradually pour the butter into the egg mixture and blend until a thickened, creamy sauce forms. Season with salt and pepper.

c) To make the eggs, prepare the spinach by sautéing it in the olive oil in a saucepan, stirring, just until wilted and still bright green. Stir in the cream, season with salt and pepper, and keep warm.

d) Heat the artichoke bottoms and keep warm.

e) Fill a skillet or shallow pot with 2 ½ inches of water. Add the vinegar and heat to medium hot.

f) One at a time, crack 4 of the eggs into a small cup and gently pour them into the water. Simmer the eggs until they rise to the top of the liquid, and then turn them over with a spoon. Cook until the whites are set but the yolks are still runny. Remove with a slotted spoon and pat dry with paper towels. Repeat with the remaining eggs.

g) Spoon a serving of the spinach on each of 4 plates. Place 2 artichoke bottoms on each plate on top of the spinach and place an egg on each artichoke. Spoon the hollandaise sauce over all and serve immediately.

CONCLUSION

In conclusion, Cajun cuisine is a rich and diverse style of cooking that has become an integral part of Louisiana's cultural heritage. It is a cuisine that reflects the history and influences of the region's diverse population, with dishes that celebrate bold flavors, hearty ingredients, and a unique blend of spices and seasonings.

Cajun cuisine is loved by people all over the world for its rich and satisfying dishes like gumbo, jambalaya, and red beans and rice. Whether enjoyed in a traditional Cajun restaurant, a food festival, or prepared at home, Cajun cuisine is sure to satisfy any craving for bold and flavorful comfort food.

With its unique blend of spices, hearty ingredients, and rich cultural heritage, Cajun cuisine has become an important part of American culinary culture, beloved by people from all walks of life. Whether exploring the tastes of the bayou for the first time or enjoying a favorite Cajun dish, this cuisine is sure to leave diners with a sense of warmth and satisfaction.

www.ingramcontent.com/pod-product-compliance
Lightning Source LLC
Chambersburg PA
CBHW070345120526
44590CB00014B/1047